World War Two

Diaries of
ACFP Geldenhuys

Preller Geldenhuys

First published in 2007 by Prop Geldenhuys
prop@peysoft.co.za
Copyright © Prop Geldenhuys 2016
Cover design by Peysoft Publishing

Printed by Lulu.com

ISBN: 978-0-9941309-4-5

Paeroa
2016

To Honour the Memory

Of my father

ACFP Geldenhuys

(also known as Preller Geldenhuys)

*There is a **right** time for everything*

A Time to be born, a Time to die

A Time for War, a Time for Peace

Ecl 3 v 1

Contents

Glossary

ABW – Anglo-Boer War

A/C – Aircraft

A-G – Air to Ground

AS – Air School

Capt - Captain

CFI – Chief Flying Instructor

EFTS – Elementary Flying Training School

ITS – Initial Training School

LG – Landing Ground

LL – Low Level

Lt - Lieutenant

Lt Col – Lieutenant Colonel

OC – Officer Commanding

SAAF – South African Air Force

S/L – Squadron Leader

Sqn – Squadron

UDI – Rhodesian Unilateral Declaration of Independence

X-C – Cross Country

ZAS – Zwartkop Air Station

Preface

This book by is about my fathers' South African Air Force service during World War Two 1939 – 1945.

He married my mother, Mathia Martha Lotter just before the war broke out – and they had the first three of four children born during the war years. The fourth child, born in Luanshya, Northern Rhodesia, did not survive.

It must have been very soon after his marriage that he joined the military, like his father Johannes Albertus and eldest brother Hendry Jacobus Geldenhuys. When he was born, he was burdened with my grandmothers family names – Abram Carl Frederick Preller Geldenhuys.

Abram Carl Frederick Preller Geldenhuys was born Bothaville, Orange Free State, South Africa, 2 August 1916 and died Pretoria, Transvaal, SA, 13 February 1972 – aged 55½ years.

His parents were Johannes Albertus Geldenhuys and Anna Elizabeth Preller – who were grain farmers on Rustpan, the family farm in the Bothaville district, on the road to Kroonstad.

He was the youngest of five children, and according to family tradition, was named after his maternal grandfather. His eldest brother was named after his paternal grandfather – Hendrik Jacobus Geldenhuys. His older sisters were named Anna Elizabeth (Bess), Lilla and Mienie.

They were initially farmed schooled and finished their Schooling at Bothaville – where my father matriculated.

My grandfather had fought against the British in the Anglo-Boer War. My father was born during the First World War – best known in South Africa as the war of Boer teen Boer en Broer teen Broer – Farmer against farmer and brother against brother. It will be recalled that Germany was very sympathetic to the South Africans during the Anglo-Boer War 1899 – 1902; thus a sizeable proportion of the population was very reluctant to take up arms to attack

German South West Africa as required by the Allies. However, young ACFP was totally oblivion to the ramifications of the First World War.

Jan A. and A.C.F.Preller GELDENHUYS
05 September 1931

However, by 1939, my both my grandfather and my uncle Hendry were in uniform, preparing for war against the might of Adolf Hitler's Germany. My Uncle Hendry, who was an Anglo-Boer War baby, was already fifteen year's my father's senior.

So it was but a question of time that my father too, would find himself in uniform.

My grandfather Jan, Uncle Henry and my father Preller Geldenhuys - 1940's Army and Air Force service during World War II

The photograph was taken while my Dad was still undergoing pilot training in order to qualify for his 'Wings'. My grandfather, who rose to Veldcornet rank during the Anglo-Boer War, seems to sport SADF Army Captain rank. Uncle Henry is showing Lieutenant rank and my father – Abram Carl Federick Preller – is still a SAAF pupil pilot.

This then is where this story starts, with initial and basic flying training in the South African Air Force, on the 5th May 1940.

SAAF Wings

A lesson in War, warrants repeating: It results in "to the Victor, the spoils". In other words, the Government in power writes its own so-called 'history'. Where this is lacking, especially in Africa, country name changes occur, followed by the hijacking of City, town and even street names. So, before long, places and names like Rhodesia and even Pretoria will fade into history.

This recollection covers my father Preller's East African Campaign and South African experiences during World War II – in forgotten Abyssinia and Eritrea.

'Prop' Preller Geldenhuys
Paeroa
New Zealand
September 201

WO Abram Carl Fredric Preller Geldenhuys

My Dad – Preller Geldenhuys

Dad attested into the South African Air Force at Roberts Heights on 5th May 1940, and served briefly at East London and Bloemfontein before joining pilot training with No 1 Elementary Flying Training School (EFTS) Baragwanath on 9th September 1940.

His flying instructor on the Tiger Moth was Lieutenant Louis Cecil 'Cookie' Botha, an acknowledged Ace fighter pilot credited with five victories and who was later awarded the Distinguished Flying Cross. Anyway, after eleven hours and twenty minutes' flying instruction, Dad went solo on 23rd September 1940.

While with No 1 EFTS, he flew his Final Test with Major Spoor, the Chief Flying Instructor - CFI (who was subsequently killed during the War), and was assessed as an Average Plus pupil pilot.

As a matter of interest, a Lieutenant Shuttleworth instructed Dad on 1st November 1940, in a Tiger, on a cross-country flown on instruments. By February 1944, Shuttleworth was a Lieutenant Colonel, commanding No 15 Squadron.

Dad was then posted to No 2 EFTS Randfontein doing conversions to the DH 82A and DH Hornet, and then posted to No 21 Air School at Kimberley to commence his Initial Training School (ITS) on Hawker Hart aircraft, and on Hind aircraft on 31st November 1940. In February of 1941, Advanced Training entailed air to ground firing and low level / high dive-bombing. Battle formations and air to air gunnery were also carried out. Warrant Officer, later Lieutenant Paddy Hope was Dad's main instructor. He also flew with Captain Quirk (also subsequently killed during the war) on solo tests on searchlight landings.

Tiger Moth – World War II Pilot Training Aircraft

Paddy Hope had a significant influence on P/P Preller Geldenhuys' flying career. His first sortie, a Hawker Hart re-familiarisation was on 3rd February 1941, followed two weeks later on quarter and stern attack instruction (for air combat survival which materialised a mere four months later). It is also evident, for whatever reason, that Paddy Hope, as Dad's instructor, completed and certified Dad's Pilots logbook that month.

Having notched up 170 flying hours, Pupil Pilot Geldenhuys qualified for the coveted South African Air Force Flying Badge (Wings) on 29th March 1941 - graduated with the rank of Sergeant Pilot and posted to the Pilots' Pool at Waterkloof Air Force Base.

The following two months were rather inactive, with very little flying, except for a posting to No 43 Squadron, Zwartkop Air Station as Warrant Officer II.

Bücker Bü-133 C "Jungmeister" Nr.802 (1939)

© Nerijus Treinys 2004

Bucker Jungmeister

 A forty-minute sortie was bummed on a Bucker Jungmeister aircraft, another forty minutes dual check in a Hawker Hind followed by a half-hour sortie in a Hawker Hartbees. The latter was with Sergeant Swart who was also later killed.

Hawker Hind

Hawker Hartbees

Hawker Hart

With 171½ flying hours' experience, the day eventually arrived for deployment to the front line in the East African Campaign. Warrant Officer Class II ACFP Geldenhuys received his posting notice - to report to No 3 Fighter Squadron stationed at Addis Ababa, Abyssinia. The first stop was No 20 SFTS, Cranborne, Salisbury, Southern Rhodesia, for battle conversion to the Harvard aircraft.

The CFI was Squadron Leader Gibb, seconded by the Royal Air Force, as part of the British Commonwealth's 'Rhodesian Air Training Group' (RATG) commitment to the war effort.

Cranborne was but one of several training centres in Rhodesia, including Thornhill and Guinea Fowl in Gwelo, Kumalo and Heany in Bulawayo, and Norton to name but a few.

The Harvard conversion took seven sorties, three duals totalling 1·30 hours, and four solos totalling 2·50 hours, over a period of four days. On the fifth day, 23rd May 1941, Dad boarded the shuttle service to East Africa. He now had less than 176 flying hours to his credit, and was considered fully proficient to do battle against Hitler's Germany and Mussolini's Italy in particular. His posting to No 3 Fighter Squadron was confirmed.

SAAF pilots Bob Preller and Oudad, ACF Preller Geldenhuys, routed via Nairobi for the East African Campaign against the Italians. They were amongst the first aircrew to go into action in Kenya, Ethiopia, Abyssinia and Eritrea.

Kenya- now Tanzania

The MAP sets the scene for the East African Campaign.

East African Campaign – Abyssinia and Eritrea theatre of War

East African Campaign

The danger signals of a forthcoming war had been sounded during the Munich Crisis in 1938. The SAAF may have lacked aircraft and immediate organisation when war broke out in September 1939. But it possessed something infinitely more valuable - spirit. A spirit of resolution, adventure and enthusiasm that was to write a remarkable page in the history of aerial warfare.

To quote from 'Per Aspera ad Astra 1920-1970', "It was the pilots, aircrews and service crews of the first squadrons to go into action in Kenya, the Sudan, Eritrea and Abyssinia who set the pattern of what was to follow. They conducted a campaign of such audacity and determination against the Italian Air Force that within a short time they had mastery of the air in East Africa. Outnumbered, operating obsolete, cumbersome aircraft against the more modern machines of their adversaries, they set about putting the Italian Air Force out of business, knowing that if they failed then the Italians had the ability to blow them out of the skies in East Africa."

When the South African Parliament voted to join the Allies and to declare war on Germany, the SAAF consisted of 150 permanent force officers, 35 cadets and 1400 men. There were three service squadrons, two of them training units and five shadow squadrons that existed only on paper. The SAAF possessed about 100 aircraft, of which 63 were obsolete general purpose Hartbees. The more modern machines were six Hurricane fighters, a Fairey Battle bomber, and a Blenheim bomber.

By early 1940 the pattern of the forthcoming struggle had become clear. The Middle East and East Africa were to become major theatres of war, emphasising that the Cape sea route would need protection to allow the safe passage of essential convoys of troops and supplies to those areas. The Italian Empire of Somaliland, Abyssinia and Eritrea would need to be contained and then dealt with before the forces established there could break out to threaten East and Central Africa.

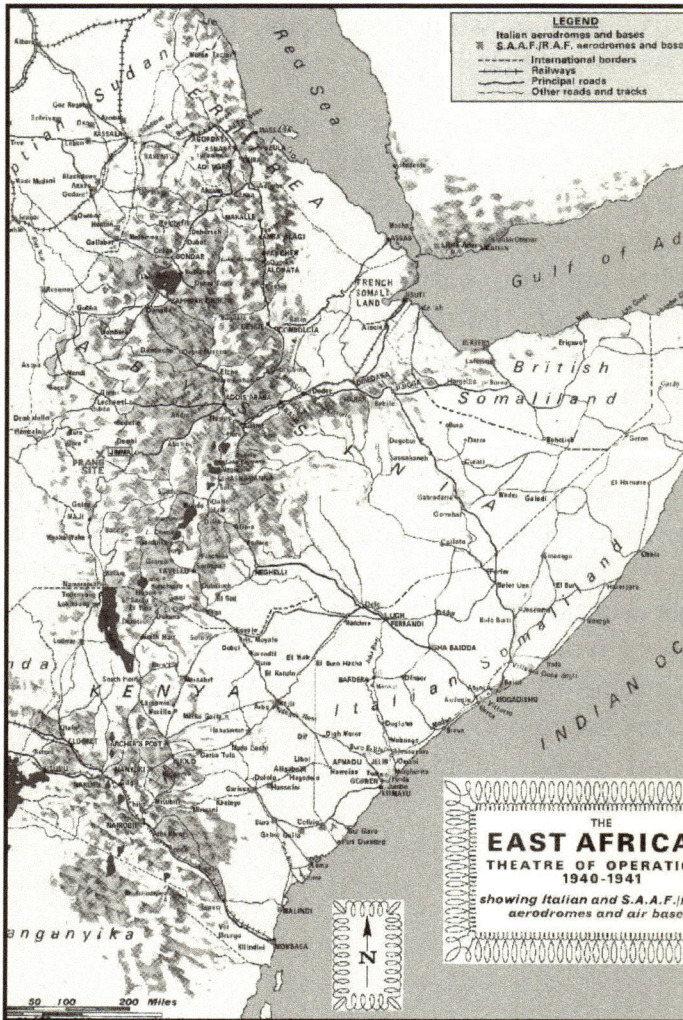

The East Africa Theatre of Operations 1940-1941, showing Italian and S.A.A.F./R.A.F. aerodromes and air bases

No 3 Squadron SAAF – World War II Theatre of Operations

In May 1940, the SAAF dispatched three squadrons to Kenya. 'A' flight of No 1 Squadron, with some Hawker Furies, went on to Egypt where they collected a number of Gloster Gladiators and later ferried some of them to Khartoum in the Sudan. The other flight of the squadron remained in Kenya, to soon become No 2 Squadron.

Later in 1940, No 3 Fighter Squadron was formed and sent to Kenya, as were two army co-operation squadrons, equipped with Hartbees (it was this Squadron that Dad was destined to join. 'A' Flight was re-equipped with Hurricanes and 'B' Flight with Gladiators).

On 10th June 1940 Italy entered the war - as predicted by Dr Gustav Preller nearly a year earlier. However, A C F Preller Geldenhuys had already joined the SAAF as a Pupil Pilot.

Lieutenant-Colonel Bob R H Preller

Bob Preller and Oudad were second cousins, with Bob being the senior by several years. 'Bob' Robert Herman's father, Robert, was a twin. His father's twin inherited the grandfather's Christian names of Mauritz Herman Otto Preller. Robert junior's great-grandfather was Carel Friedrick Preller, which were also Oudad's middle names, from the same great-grandfather.

In 1934-35, the SAAF sent its first two officers to Britain to study. Captain Tasker to the Flying and Armaments School; Lieutenant R H 'Bob' Preller to the Engineering School. They returned to initiate training in these subjects. This was thus the beginning of the modernisation of the SAAF. By 1939, Robert Herman Preller was promoted to Captain, and shortly thereafter to Major.

On 6th March, Captain R H Preller carried out "handling and landing practice" on Hurricane L1708 assembled in Durban. The following day, Preller thrilled the country by flying the Hurricane to Waterkloof in 73 minutes at 265 mph. *The Star* printed the two bladed Hurricanes in its newspaper, as did author James Ambrose Brown, in his historical account of the campaigns of the SAAF in Italian East Africa June 1940 - November 1941, titled *"A Gathering of Eagles"*. This feat has gone down in history as the SAAFs first Hurricane to arrive at Waterkloof, Pretoria.

The S.A.A.F.'s first Hurricane at Waterkloof, Pretoria, March 1939. Piloted from Cape Town by Captain R. H. Preller, average speed 276 m.p.h.　　　(*The Star*.)

Bob Preller's Hurricane

On 12th June 1940, only two days after Italy declared war, Major R H Preller, led the first offensive and photographic reconnaissance out over the Italian Somaliland wasteland of the Northern Frontier District. The purpose was to locate enemy aerodromes near the Kenyan border, and to attack enemy landing grounds within 25 miles of Colbio. The three Hartbees of No 11 Squadron (being one of the three original squadrons that the SAAF had earlier dispatched to Kenya) made this incursion with orders to attack all military objectives with bombs and machine-guns. They flew from Nairobi, leaving behind the rich farmlands of central Kenya, to Garissa where they refuelled before traversing the waterless bush and semi-desert, nearly 300 miles in depth, of the Northern Frontier District (the Italian sector of East Africa). Here certain focal points were important because of the water supply they afforded. At Wajir, a squalid Somali village with Indian dukas and a mud-brick fortress, 'C' Flight No 237 (Rhodesia) Squadron, RAF was operating.

Beyond Wajir lay the wasteland of thorn bush and scrub which divided the British forces from the Italians; it was across this territory that the Hartbees of the SAAF now ventured. They were Nos 864, 804, 856; their crews, Major Preller and

Air Corporal B Ackerman, 2nd Lieutenant P Robbertse and Air Corporal P Sewell; 2nd Lieutenant B Hutchinson and Air Sergeant L Feinberg. Theirs were the first South African eyes to look on the coming area of battle in Jubaland.

It was against Wajir that the Italians made their first aerial attack on a forward air base in Kenya. On 13th June, three Italian Caproni 133's attacked No 237 (Rhodesia) Squadron, damaging two Hardys, sent the entire 5,000 gallon aviation fuel stock up in a blaze; killed five and wounded a pilot officer and eleven Askaris of the King's African Rifles (Note: KAR=RAR). The next day (14th June) the puny Hartbees biplanes of No 11 Squadron were sent out to attack the wireless station, barracks and petrol dumps at Bardera. Their mission was a success, as was a raid by Ju 86 bombers of No 12 Squadron the following day over the Italian aerodromes at Kismayu, Jelib and Afmadu in Somaliland.

ITALIAN BOMBER CAPRONI CA 133

Italian Caproni 133

These SAAF initiatives were somewhat of an impertinence considering the relative sizes of the warring factions. In all, there were only about forty SAAF aircraft in Kenya, lined up against an estimated three hundred IAF (more properly named Regia Aeronautica) aircraft, albeit that they were spread over the length and breadth of the Italian Empire, embracing Somaliland, Abyssinia and Eritrea.

To reach their targets the pilots of No 11 Squadron would leave their bases in the Kenya Highlands and refuel at advance fields in the bush, often sleeping out for the night under the wings of their aircraft before taking off at first light. They would often refuel at Wajir on the outward flight and at Habaswein on the return. This sustained programme of air attacks was continued ruthlessly, smashing planes on the ground, and damaging aerodromes, railways, and transport and fuel stocks.

On 18th June, Major Bob Preller, commanding No 11 Squadron in Kenya, had been informed that his squadron would be handing over the Hartbees it had been using as bombers and would re-arm with dive-bombers. Preller's pilots were to be trained on the Fairey Battle operating from Archer's Post. The Battle could carry 1,000 pounds of bombs for a thousand miles at a speed of 240 mph. It brought within range Mogadishu, the Somaliland seaport where Marshal Graziani had landed his invasion troops in 1935, and made possible raids on Shashamanna, deep in Abyssinia.

However, before Major Preller could return to the Union to re-equip his squadron, he had been ordered on a special reconnaissance to photograph landing grounds in the vicinity of Kismayu harbour and district. With his crew of Air Corporals E Pettersen and B Ackerman, he took off in Battle 901 on 19th June - and did not return. It was surmised that he had landed at one of the advanced operational fields. An extensive search continued each day until 27th June, without being posted 'officially missing'. Lieutenant Colonel S A Melville, OC 1st Bomber Brigade, reasoned that owing to the faulty communications in the territory, and to the fact that the Italians had not claimed the Battle as a casualty, there was still hope that the crews had landed in some inaccessible place and would turn up, as others had done.

This was the first Fairey Battle to arrive at Zwartkop Air Station, Pretoria, in May 1939. There is also an all-wood, prototype model Hurricane on the left – the type flown by Bob Preller.

A Fairey Battle – Fighter Bomber

When on 27th June nothing had been reported, Major Preller and his crew became the first South African airmen posted "officially" missing. On 1 July, Pilot Officer Hutchinson of the Rhodesian Air Force, on a routine dawn patrol of the Garissa-

Liboi road, spotted a lone European in khaki accompanied by two Somalis jogging slowly in the direction of Liboi. He dropped the message, 'Raise your arms if you need help'. The man on the camel responded.

This was Major Preller. At sundown a truck from the King's African Rifles and an ambulance arrived. Preller, weak, suffering severe sunburn, with blistered feet, told the rescuers that his crew could be found at a waterhole 12 miles on the enemy side of the border. Exhausted by seven days without food and four without water, the NCOs had been ordered to remain at the waterhole for three days and attempt to recover their strength before pushing on. Preller told his rescuers that he had set off with the intention of photographing Afmadu on the outward trip. When nearly there he observed cloud formations in the vicinity of the more dangerous area at Kismayu. Intending to use these as cover for his photographing of that area he arrived over Kismayu harbour at about 10,000 feet. Two enemy warships in the bay fired on him. He then flew north-east to Margherita further up the coast, and turned inland towards Afmadu where he made a low-level attack on an Italian plane on the airfield. On his second pass the Battle was hit in the radiator by a single bullet, probably fired from a rifle. A jet of glycol and steam blew into the aircraft, forcing the observer and gunner to hang over the side to breathe. Major Preller dived the machine to keep the engine cool. Twelve miles from the enemy airfield the engine seized. The sturdy Battle sheered through the branches of big trees and came to rest. Preller's only injury was a gash on the forehead from the gunsight.

The three men removed the compass, soaked a parachute in petrol, spread it over the aircraft and, having set it alight, turned south with the Lewis gun and one water bottle between them. (Standing orders were that all aircraft were to carry rations, water and rifles). They soon discarded the Lewis gun but kept a Very pistol to signal search planes. They suffered intensely. Once they came on a mud-hole covered with green slime, stripped naked and wallowed in the cool mud. Filling the water bottle with slime they managed to distil a few mouthfuls of drinking water in a funnel made of photographic film . . . . stark naked and caked with mud they staggered on, carrying their clothing until the mud dried off.

Preller described the torment of thirst. "You lose all sense of everything - even vision - you feel like biting into your own flesh to draw some moisture." He and Ackerman chewed the pulpy leaves of aloes - only to suffer greater torment. The airmen smashed the compass to get to the fluid inside. The alcohol was impossible to swallow so they mixed it with urine in the water bottle and wet their mouths. By that time, Air Corporal Ackerman had lost so much weight it was possible to see the screws sticking out of his skin from a metal plate in his arm. Finally Major Preller went on alone in an effort to reach the border: Twenty seven miles from it, he encountered two Somalis who put him on a camel and led him in. Later the Somalis led a patrol of the King's African Rifles into enemy territory to find the missing men. They were alive at the waterhole and on 4th July - fifteen days after they had been shot down - were brought in.

Although one roll of film taken on the flight had been destroyed, Air Corporal Pettersen had kept the other intact. On 9th October 1940 an immediate award of the DFC was made to Major Preller - the first SAAF decoration of the War - for imbuing his squadron with his own offensive spirit and bringing back a very valuable exposed film of enemy military objectives. His comrades were both mentioned in dispatches.

Pretoria to Nairobi Route

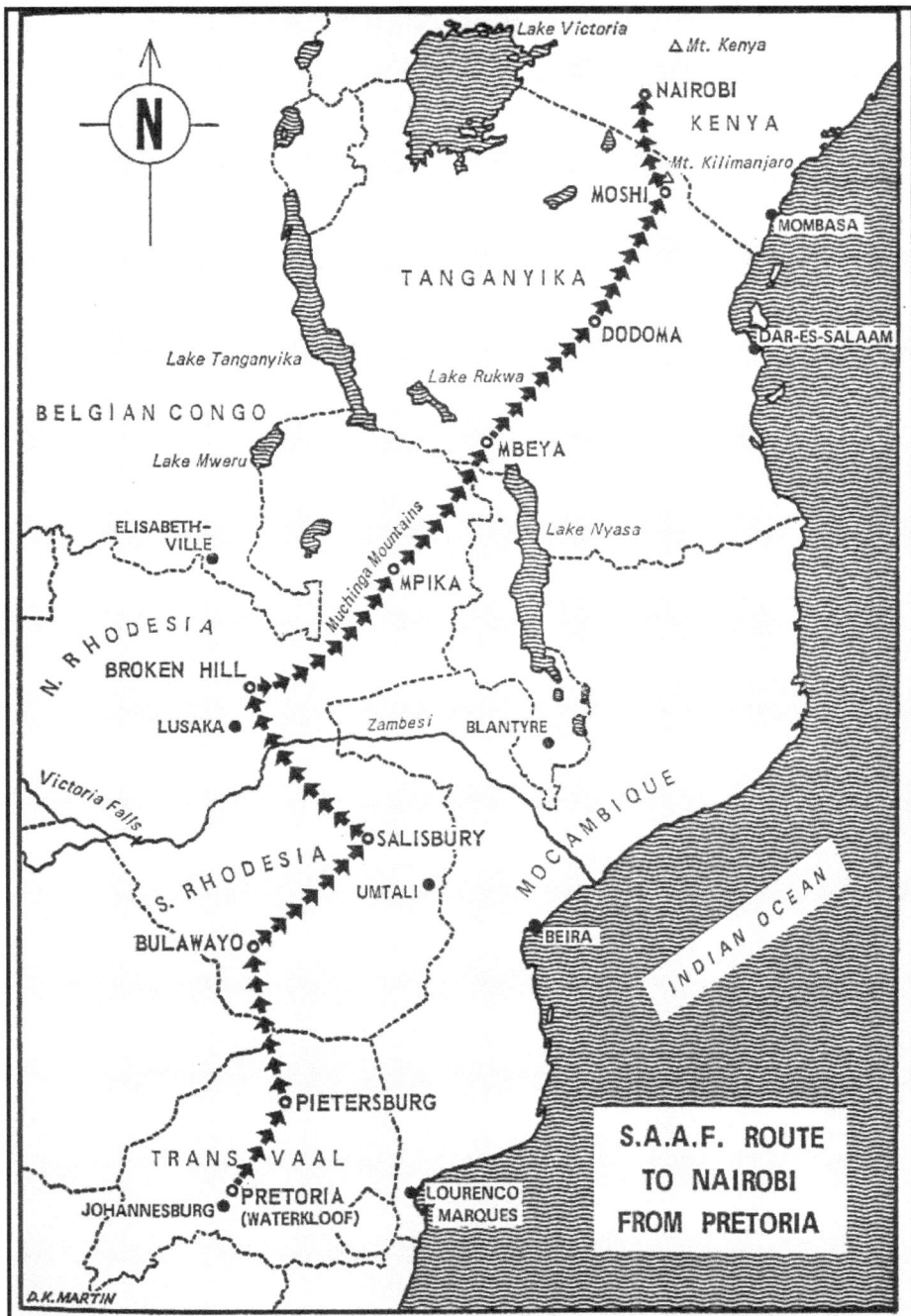

N

Lake Victoria △ Mt. Kenya

NAIROBI
KENYA
Mt. Kilimanjaro
MOSHI
MOMBASA

TANGANYIKA
DODOMA
DAR-ES-SALAAM

Lake Tanganyika
Lake Rukwa

BELGIAN CONGO
Lake Mweru
MBEYA
Lake Nyasa

ELISABETH-
VILLE
Muchinga Mountains
MPIKA

N. RHODESIA
BROKEN HILL
LUSAKA
Zambesi
BLANTYRE

Victoria Falls
SALISBURY
UMTALI
MOÇAMBIQUE

S. RHODESIA
BEIRA
INDIAN OCEAN
BULAWAYO

PIETERSBURG

TRANSVAAL
PRETORIA
(WATERKLOOF)
JOHANNESBURG
LOURENCO
MARQUES

S.A.A.F. ROUTE
TO NAIROBI
FROM PRETORIA

D.K.MARTIN

27

PORT SUDAN

Atbara

Anglo-Egyptian Sudan

Red Sea

Keren

KHARTOUM
Gordon's Tree

Kassala Agordat Massawa

Asmara

Wadi Medani Azaza Barentu

Gedaref **Eritrea**

Kosti

Ma,Kalie

Gallabat Gondar Alomata Assab Aden Socotra

Azozo

Roseires Lake Tana **French Somaliland** Gulf of Aden

Kurmuk Dessie Jibuti

Comboicia Alscia

Malakal Diredawa Berbera

Addis Ababa Harar Hargeisa **British Somaliland**

Miesso Jijigga

Awash Daghabur Awareh

Jimma Algato

The Lakes Gorrahai

Soddau Shashamana **Abyssinia**

Gardula

Yavello Neghelli

Lokitaung Mega **Italian Somaliland**

Moyale

Lodwar

Uganda Marsabit El Wak Bardera

Wajir Mogadishu

Ndege's Nest

Kenya Dif

Isiolo Gobwen Indian Ocean

Lake Victoria Kisumu Nanyuki Garissa

Bura KISMAYU

Nairobi
Eastleigh

Tanganyika Mombasa

Insert

Mombasa Island

Port Reitz Mombasa Harbour

Kilindini Harbour

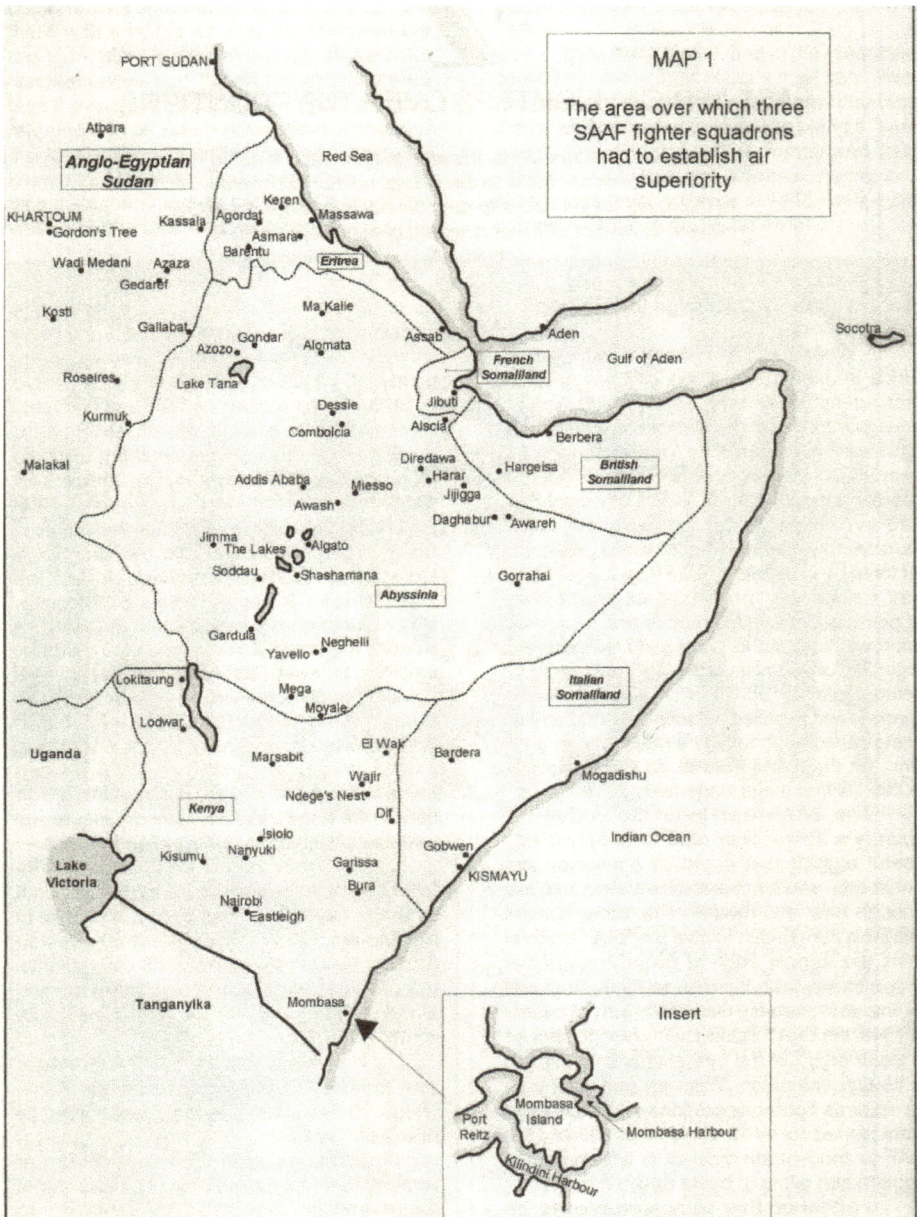

By the time Major Preller returned to duty, twenty-one members of the No 11 Squadron had returned to South Africa (22 June) to fetch the Battles. On 10th July, Preller followed to organise their flight to Kenya. By 12th August, fifteen Battles were established at Archer's Post. During the period he was missing the battle for Moyale had begun. It was to be the only Italian success of the war on this front.

Towards the end of 1940, the SAAF Squadrons had established themselves at strategic places in Kenya, carrying out softening up programmes preparatory to the invasion of Italian-held territory

Months later when the SAAF occupied the Italian airfield at Mogadishu, Preller found the remains of Battle 901 in a shed. The interior of the bomber was totally burnt out. The only identifiable thing remaining was the copper number plate of the Merlin engine. The Italians had misidentified the Battle as a "Wellesley". Their note on the machine read: 'velivolo Sud Africa Wickers Wellesley abbatutto dat (?) dubatto d'Afmudu 19 Ciugno 1940 XVII' (the Roman 17 numerals referring to the 17th year of Fascism).

By February 1941, the SAAF commenced occupying Italian aerodromes in Somaliland. As the bomber squadrons prepared to move forward, shortages of transport became the main concern. In 1965, when interviewed at Pelindaba, Preller recalled the sight of "whole formations of trucks crashing through the bush roads - the squadrons top-heavy with transport, had great trouble in concealing and organising these into convoys". The aircraft flew to the new landing grounds. No 12 Squadron had barely touched down at Gobwen on 23 February when it was re-routed to Margherita - arriving at the abandoned Italian airfield to find it in the possession of hyenas which cackled hideously in the bush. The airmen slept under the wings of the Junkers in the humid nights at that low altitude, and swam in the tepid Juba River.

Advance over the desert of the Central Ogaden followed in March 1941. The SAAF needed to cross the desert for their move into the hinterland. The airmen's convoy took three days to cross the desert to Daghabur. Major Preller recalled the scene: "How our colossal convoys found their way between Gorrahai and Daghabur is still a puzzle to me. . .

when I flew over this world I saw the 'road' expanded in some places to four or five miles wide through the sand as each driver tried to find a new path for himself.." It was desert, the sand deep and fine as powder, and the heat stunning. Convoys crawled through the bush at a snails pace, covered in a pall of dust and spread out like a great herd of beasts. Tall twirling dust devils stormed across the plains, corkscrewing up to the heavy clouds. Men were now accustomed to an issue of half a gallon of water a day.

Jijigga, with its surrounding huge areas of flat country, was virtually a natural airfield. The risk to No 2 Wing, now commanded by Lieutenant Colonel R H Preller, lay in the fact that in deciding to concentrate bombers there they exposed them to attack from Diredawa, Addis Ababa and smaller airfields even closer. The Italians had not yet abandoned Diredawa. Anti-aircraft guns still heavily defended it, and it remained operative for Savoias even after SAAF squadrons came forward to Jijigga, less than 100 miles away.

After a discussion with Lieutenant Colonel Preller, Brigadier H Daniel agreed that only communications and reconnaissance aircraft should use the old Italian fields. The remaining squadrons were to be well dispersed, the Hurricanes on the right side of the road and in the lee of the mountains, the Junkers 86s on the east side of the village, seven miles from the Daghabur road, and the Battles alongside the Hargiesa road. This dispersal was instrumental in saving the bomber force from being involved in the attacks that followed. The Italians, using Addis Ababa as base, took their opportunity after the fall of Marda Pass.

Preller's bombers began a series of operations against the lines of communication - battering at the road and railway systems. Battles and Junkers picked up fighter escorts from Daghabur over Jijigga and roared on to their targets in the vital complex around Diredawa. Here, the road from Berbera and the only railway line into Abyssinia from Jibuti, met, and followed the same route towards the capital. The route was vital to the movement of Italian troops and supplies. Diredawa itself was an important garrison town with large stores. Behind the screen of troops at Marda Pass there was much activity and the SAAF began to attack it even before the Marda Pass was abandoned. With the forward movement of Advanced Air Headquarters, No 2 Wing and No 12 Squadron, from Gorrahai to Jijigga, on 23rd and 26th March, the SAAF was now in its most advanced positions since the February offensive began.

Three days later, the Italians carried out their second attack on Jijigga - with impetuosity and daring, at 07h00, just as most of the SAAF crews were having breakfast, the fighter pilots shaving or eating at the officers' mess tent a mile away from their aircraft. Standby Captain Theron and Lieutenant Venter scrambled their Hurricanes to intercept the Italian Fiats. Theron was scarcely airborne when his Hurricane stopped a bullet in the glycol pipe, forcing him to make for the landing ground with two Fiats on his tail. The Italians followed him down, firing all the time, riddling his machine. Though Theron suffered a splinter wound above the knee he landed and made a run for it. Watchers saw him halt, bullets literally throwing dirt in his face. . and then run on, unhurt. His machine blazed so fiercely that Lieutenant Colonel Preller, watching from the main field, feared that the Italians had caught all four Hurricanes still not airborne and destroyed them.

Venter, meanwhile, was able to down one Fiat. The other two Hurricanes were able to get airborne, with a Captain Frost claiming a Fiat as well. The SAAF lost a Valentia, a Junkers 52 and a Hartbees - and 12·7mm damage to another Ju 52, which was hit from the previous raid.

It is evident that by April, a period of transition found the SAAF battle-weary. Top-level anxiety about morale and health is seen in a report made on 30th April by medical officers of No 2 Wing. Sent to the Officer Commanding, Colonel R H Preller DFC, it stated that 20 to 25% of all ranks required hospital treatment or investigation such as could be obtained in a general hospital. The health of a further 20 to 25%, due to the rigours of the campaign or illness contracted during its course, was definitely below the standard required to perform their duties adequately and continually. The majority of the remainder had deteriorated in general health. The medical officers recommended a period of complete rest and a correct diet, before embarking on a further campaign in some other theatre of war. The men were operationally tired and needed leave. Because No 2 Wing was operating over 1,000 miles away from Nairobi, it was not possible to send the men back to the Union. Instead, some were able to scrounge time off - or R&R as it is called nowadays - to Mombasa, they were sent off with instructions to make their own way back.

In April-May, Hardys, Lysanders and Gladiators of No 237 (Rhodesia) Squadron repeatedly machine-gunned Amba Alagi, Fort Toselli and the Folaga Pass. The attack on Fort Tolelli on 14th May was the last operation of the Rhodesian squadron. On 20th May orders were issued for its transfer to Wadi Halfa in Egypt.

During May-June 1941, inclement weather adversely affected air operations. The weather, with lashing rain and violent thunderstorms bursting over mountain and forest, was such that of twelve pilots' reports made on a single day (11 May) ten mentioned the weather hazard. In addition, No 3 Squadron top ace Captain J E Frost was flown to Nairobi for an emergency operation on 20th May 1941. He was the SAAF's top scoring ace of the East African campaign with a total of forty-nine and five-sixths aircraft - including fifteen and one third destroyed in combat, five probable; nine damaged; and twenty-five destroyed on the ground. Captain Frost then returned to the Union (on 23rd July 1941 he was given command of No 5 Squadron at Swartkop Air Station - and by mid-December, with the rank of Major, he was deployed to the Middle East).

For the record, Lieutenant Colonel R H Preller DFC was the wartime Commanding Officer of No 12 Squadron from September to November 1941. He took over from Major J B Botes, and handed over command of the Squadron to Lieutenant Colonel S L Bosch AFC. All the subsequent commands were also of relatively short wartime duration. That is, Bosch November 41 to January 42; Maj. J J Nash January 42 to March 42; Lieutenant Colonel H J Martin DFC March 42 to July 42; Lt Col F A Hofmeyr July 42 to January 43; Lt Col F L Kotze DFC January 43 to August 43; Lt Col O F Wellington DFC August 43 to January 44; Lt Col M Barnby DFC January 44 to July 44; Lt Col F J Burniaux DFC July 44 to September 44, and Lt Col Coull DFC September 44 to 45. Permit me to digress for one brief moment. Some thirty years later, while Commandant Gerry Coetzee commanded No 12 Squadron, they, together with No 5 Squadron (Canberras) of the Rhodesian Air Force, conducted strategic photographic missions in Zambia, Zaire and Mozambique – when "Prop" Preller Matt Geldenhuys was the 'A' Flight Commander.

The time had arrived for newly qualified 'replacement' aircrews to report for duty in the East African theatre of operations that were advancing northwards and westwards from captured Regia Aeronautica - IAF - Italian Air Force bases. For Warrant Officer Class II Geldenhuys, A C F P, it was time to fight battles against the Italians..

Go North, Young Man, Go North

WO II Preller Geldenhuys enjoyed his last solo flight in Harvard N7131 on 22nd May 1941. The sortie lasted 1.05 hours - nearly double the time of the previous six sorties flown from Cranborne, (Salisbury, Rhodesia). The next day he boarded the Sir John Craddock for East Africa. Italy was the birthplace of Fascism. Mussolini had sided with Germany's Adolf Hitler and his Nazism. Dad was about to take on the full force of the Italians in Abyssinia.

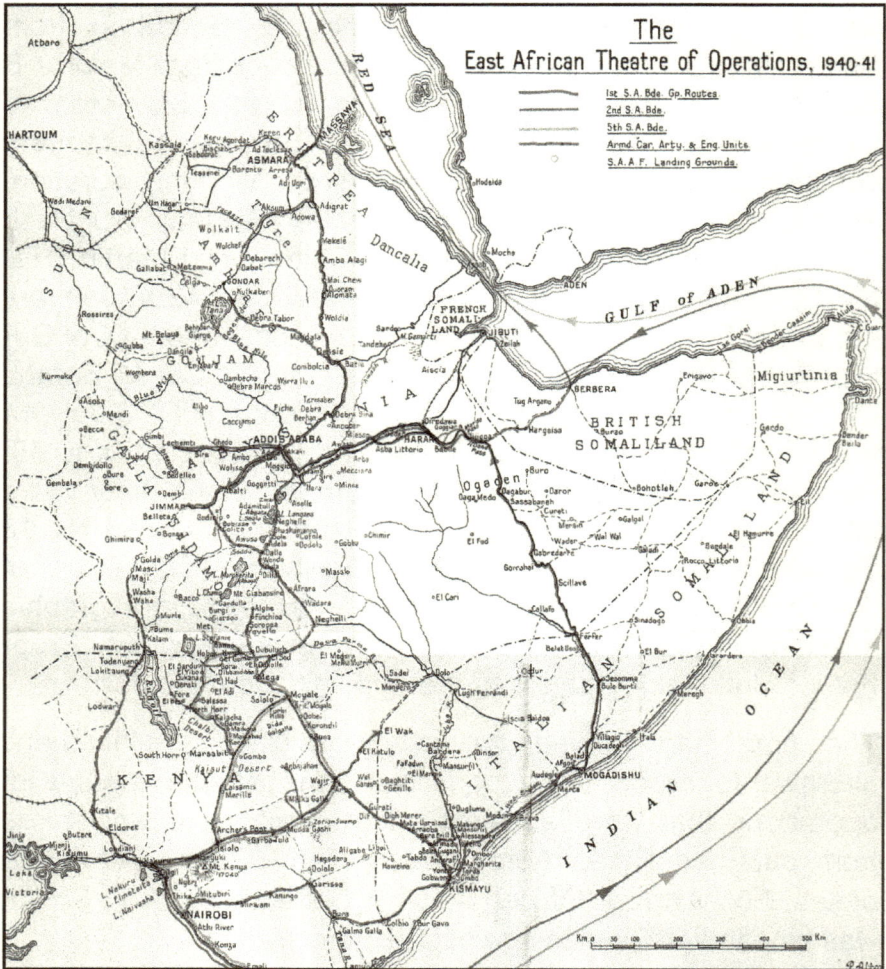

The East African Theatre of Operations, 1940-41

The Sir John Craddock was a Lodestar aircraft, piloted by Lieutenant Parsons of No 50 Squadron. It was only towards the end of 1940 that the Lodestars were obtained from the American Air Force to supplement the appropriated Junkers airliners of South African Airways to ply the route between Germiston and Nairobi.

Lodestar

It was a long day - the Sir John Craddock took off from Salisbury at midday, flew for 1.10 hours to Lusaka for a brief refuel. They then left for Mbeya in south-west Tanganyika, flew to Mpika along the Muchinga Mountains of Northern Rhodesia, - arriving at 17h05. Mbeya lies between Lake Nyasa (now Malawi) and Lake Rukwa. Lake Tanganyika, part of the Great Rift Valley, lay further over to the west, and Dad vowed to visit the impressive lakes, God willing.

The next day, after a leisurely breakfast, and approximately mid-morning, Lieutenant Parsons took to the air again from Mbeya with his northbound passengers, and stopped very briefly during the lunch hour at Dodoma in central Tanganyika. Departure was at half past one for the comfortable two and a quarter hour flight to Nairobi in Kenya, passing the Roof of Africa en route - the majestic Mount Kilimanjaro that towers to 19,340 feet above sea level.

Nairobi was the major staging post for the Shuttle Service up to North Africa and the East African war theatres. In addition, it is here that the South Africans had the foresight to plan their offensive operations against the Italian Empire. The SAAF had, in the last days of May 1941, lost many of its most experienced pilots, as well as many of its operationally serviceable aircraft. Indeed, loss of pilots of the likes of Captains Frost, Clyde-Morley and Lieutenant Venter of No 3 Squadron, Lieutenant Steyn and an Air Sergeant of No 15 Squadron, and Captain Giles of No 41 Squadron could ill be afforded at this crucial time. The two replacement pilots, of whom Dad was one, had just arrived in a nick of time.

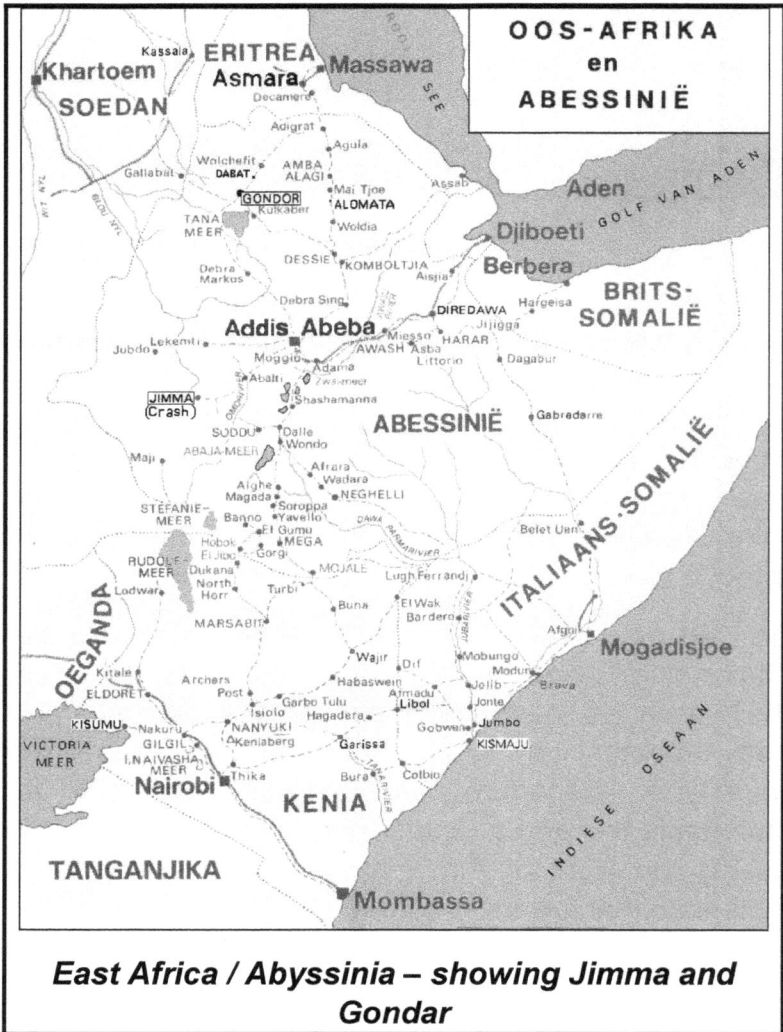

East Africa / Abyssinia – showing Jimma and Gondar

Ten days later, on 3rd June 1941, after extensive briefings and war preparations, the time had come to conclude the journey to East Africa - in a Junkers 52 piloted by Lieutenant Marshall. The Ju 52s, like the Ju 86s, had been inherited from South African Airways - the former as transport aircraft and the latter as bombers or coastal patrol aircraft.

To say that the 3rd June was a long day is an understatement. Take-off was at 07h15 followed by four long hours to Lugh Ferrandi airfield in Somalia for a refuelling stop. Lugh Ferrandi is due north-east from Nairobi, on the fringe of the Abyssinia desert, and on the banks of the Juba River. The airfield had been bombed by Major Preller's No 11 Squadron in August 1940 - using three Fairy Battles. The town was subsequently captured and occupied in early March 1941, by light forces of the 12th African Division. The enemy, the Italian 101st Division was ordered by Lieutenant General Pietro Gazzera (Supreme Commander of the Italians) to retire and to join forces with him at Neghelli. A two and a half hour lunch and refuel stop, plus leg stretch, were taken. Then all aboard at 13h45 for the final leg.

The next gruelling four and a quarter hours trip to Diredawa, directly due north of Lugh Ferrandi, over a vast interior desert, must have been a formidable sight. Diredawa had fallen only three months earlier on about 28th March. Harar, on precipitous passes between Diredawa and Jijigga, was another fantastic sight, with its wild mountainous country, steep slopes, precipices and rushing torrents. The road, magnificently engineered, clung to the high slopes, gradually descending to Diredawa. The Italians had blown down cliffs in many places and demolished bridges. Spending over eight hours in the air is a long day in any pilot's book. Addis Ababa, the capital, lay another 270 miles further west, where the Jibuti harbour railway line ended.

Warrant Officer Class II A C F Preller Geldenhuys had arrived in East Africa to make his contribution to the SAAF war effort in World War II.

Abyssinia (later Ethiopia)

An overland trip from Diredawa to Addis Ababa followed, to where 'B' Flight of No 3 Fighter Squadron was established. Addis Ababa, the capital of Abyssinia, was to become a major staging post to and from numerous detachments. In any event, it became 'home' till mid June (the 17th) 1941 - and consisted of one major event - familiarisation with the Gloster Gladiator. The Gladiator was a highly manoeuvrable biplane fighter capable of a top speed of 407 km/h (253 mph) and powered by an enormous Bristol Mercury radial engine. This was a far cry from the de Havilland Tiger Moth with its in-line Gypsy Major engine and cruising speed of 129 km/h (80 mph).

Gloster Gladiator

But pilots the world over, please consider - the familiarisation sortie was only of thirty minutes duration. And without the benefit of dual instruction; from an unfamiliar airfield in a foreign country; the previous self-piloted sortie was carried out at Cranborne twenty three days earlier and the next sortie would only be a further two weeks hence, and then only with 175 hours logged. Think of flying currency in a modern context. For militiamen, think of the saying of "hurry up and wait - it should have been done yesterday". What a thirty-minute familiarisation to type that must have been.

I for one can imagine how the first pre-flight briefing had gone. The Flight Commander was Captain Peter Hayden-Thomas. It must have been something like this:

> Flight Commander: "There is a Gladiator. Get yourself airborne."
>
> Dad apprehensively: "Who will teach me to fly it?"
>
> Hayden-Thomas: "Don't be an ass. How can anyone teach you when there's only one cockpit? Just get in and do a few circuits and bumps and you will soon get the hang of it. You had better get all the practice you can because the next thing you know you'll be dicing in the air with some clever little Italian who will be trying to shoot you down."
>
> Dad, thinking: "Surely, this is not the right way of doing things. They had spent eight months and a great deal of money training me to fly and suddenly that was the end of it all."
>
> Hayden-Thomas: "We have just lost our most experienced pilots. We don't have the resources - the life expectancy on a fighter squadron can be rather short. It is a case of every man for himself."
>
> Dad (hesitantly):   "Oh well. I have studied the pilot's notes. Here goes. Wish me luck as you wave me good-bye."

Dad (on landing):   "I made it. That was not too bad". Then thinking aloud 'Nobody is going to teach me air-to-air combat in this over extended operational squadron. I have been pushed into the deep end. It is a case of 'sink or swim."

Dad (5 months later): "I survived only by the skin of my teeth."

The Gladiators were up against slightly superior Fiats - designated CR 42 - single seat, single engine biplanes, capable of 270 mph at 13,100 feet (versus the Gladiator's 245 mph at 15,000 feet), and armed with 2 x 12·7mm cannon (versus ·303 guns). The Gladiator was armed with the two fixed machine guns, and these actually fired rounds through the revolving propeller. The firing mechanism was seen as the greatest piece of magic, to permit two machine-guns firing thousands of rounds a minute, synchronised to fire through the propeller revolving at thousands of revs a minute without hitting the propeller blades. It had something to do with a little oil pipe and that the propeller shaft communicated with the machine guns by sending pulses along the pipe to trigger firing.

All Smiles - with First Solo

Dad was allocated Gladiator 2283, but foul weather set in, virtually grounding air support for the next two weeks. Jimma was taken early in June 1941. The picture of that week's action is one of a hidden enemy - of deep wooded gorges, of twisting narrow roads flanked by mountains which made dive-bombing a nightmare - of occasional glimpses of transport, hidden or on the move to Jimma. The Italians hit back from nests of anti-aircraft guns. Puffs of pinkish or black smoke showed the calibre of the guns being used. Captain G A Giles of No 41 Squadron fell victim while circling to observe and bomb artillery positions. He spun in, killing both himself and his observer, Sergeant MacMillan. It was a battle fought in atrocious weather, 7/8ths cloud at 500 feet and lashing rain, flown off sodden airfields by pilots on short rations. Sometimes the bombers were led to their targets by the white puffs of smoke shells fired by the artillery, sometimes the Gladiators circled first and dived to mark the positions of hidden men and guns. Artillery men, high on the escarpment, which was in some places between 3,000 and 5,000 feet in height, could look down from their observation posts and actually see the aircraft bombing far below them.

Once across the Omo at Abalti and Sciola, the 22nd East African Brigade pushed west towards Jimma and the 23rd Nigerian Brigade towards Lechemti. It was to Jimma and Lechemti that WO II Geldenhuys was tasked to escort a Colonel.

That first mission was eventful. Dad escorted Colonel Stallard, flying in a De Havilland Dragon Rapide, from Jimma to Addis Ababa on 26th June. This entailed a 1.25 hour sortie, flying south-west for some 200 miles, with a 17h00 take-off. Then on the following day, after an early start, to Lechemti, and return to Addis Ababa after two and half hours escort duty. After a quick turn-round (i.e. refuel and re-arm if necessary), it was airborne at 11h15 to return to Jimma. Then the bad news followed.

On landing, Gladiator 2283 'arrived' - crash landing and ending up inverted with the port wing being torn from the wing root and bottom port wing drooping rather sadly at an acute anhedral angle. In addition, the starboard wings also looked pretty sick - the bottom wing resembling the Ju 87 Stuka profile and top wing torn from the fuselage at its rear spar attachment. From the curvature of the propeller at impact, it was obvious that power was applied. Gloster Gladiator 2283 was no more - the date, 27th June, 1941.

.. WOII ACFP Geldenhuys crashed on landing at Jimma: a/s, wing and tail damaged. 1th July 1941

Gladiator Prang at Jimma by Ou Dad Geldenhuys

In all fairness, it needs to be said that cognisance be given to several facts. Jimma had just fallen. Dad was probably one of the first allied aircraft that landed at this previously held Italian airfield. The weather was foul, runways probably waterlogged, with strong crosswinds.

So June ended, a total of four solo sorties totalling nearly six hours. Captain Peter Hayden-Thomas certified Dad's logbook in his capacity as "Officer Commanding 'B' Flight, No 3 Squadron. But, more about this gentleman a little later on, when he was shot down - not once, but twice. I think my interpretation of Dad's first pre-flight briefing could indeed have been very realistic.

Captain Clyde-Morley, the 'A' Flight Commander disappeared on a patrol over Jimma on 29th May, shot down by ground fire. Lieutenant A S Venter, sent to search for him, found that the flight commander had forced landed, but a few days later, he was killed. Lieutenant Venter was sent on a patrol from Addis Ababa but failed to arrive at Algato (he had crashed 15 miles south of Soddu) Captain G Giles, a veteran pilot, of No 41

Squadron, at age 43 the oldest SAAF combat pilot, was killed on 5th June. When the South Africans first flew in to Combolcia and Dessie, three Hartbees and two Gladiators came to grief on their first landings. Even the Italians had recently lost three Fiats, which had flipped on their backs and crashed.

On the 24th, pilots were briefed that the Free Belgian forces were moving eastwards from Bambela (making Italian retreat impossible).

On June 26th, No 16 Squadron (under Lieutenant Colonel Preller), machine-gunned transport in the Jubdo or Yubdo area - the squadron recorded an intercepted radio message which quoted General De Simone's admission of the great success of the air raid (De Simone's headquarters withdrew to the Indaina River).

On 27th June, a Hartbees of No 41 Squadron circled Dembi and reported low level resistance - resulting in the fall of Dembi and with it, General Nam. The same day, Junkers set ablaze a petrol lorry at Gimbi. The flames destroyed a wooden bridge over the Ulmaia River. As Dad was in the immediate vicinity, I can only guess that he, with Colonel Stallard, were eyewitnesses to all these happenings. I presume their morale must have been sky high.

Listening to the Gramophone (ancient version of modern CD)

On Stand-by: Awaiting Scramble Call-out

Other events between 24th and 27th June 1941 were as follows: General Gazzera surrendered at Dembidollo on 6th

July 1941. Resistance of the East African Empire was thus concentrated in the Gondar region. Here, until November, Lieutenant General Guglielmo Nasi, with a stout heart, 25,000 troops, a few aircraft, had a tenuous air link with Italy. The torrential rains over the next three months turned his fortress crags into moated castles, and while he waited for the attacks that were to come from all points of the compass, his men dug ever-deeper tunnels and caves to protect them from air attack. General Nasi had commanded the invasion of British Somaliland; thereafter, he was sent to Gondar to establish the Italian stronghold.

Combolcia (11 July to 1 August 1941)

Alomata, 120 miles from Gondar, was being prepared for the SAAF in the heart of bandit-infested country. Till this was useable, bombers and escorts were sent to use Combolcia's dangerous mountain-grit aerodrome. Despite the torrential rains during the month, on 11th July, three Junkers 86s of No 16 Squadron and three Gladiators (Captain Lucas, WO II Preller Geldenhuys plus one), of 'B' Flight of No 3 Fighter Squadron landed there. They prepared to make their first attack on Gondar on 14 July 1941.

Gondar stands about 7,000 feet above sea level amid mountains, which rise about it on three sides to heights of between 10,000 and 13,000 feet. On the south the plateau falls off towards Lake Tana, some 20 miles distant. The district had been a fortress region for centuries - at one time the inner citadel of the ancient rulers of Ethiopia, accessible only by one or two roads that zigzagged up mountainsides of incredible precipitous ness. The area was heavily timbered, its valleys fertile and its peaks within sight of Lake Tana. This watershed area was the source of the Blue Nile and in the rainy months could be approached only by air. Gondar was protected at every point of access by fortified areas - such as Wolchefit, Kulkaber, Azozo and Ambazzo. A CA 133 and two CR 42s were so skilfully camouflaged with netting, in a niche, dug out in a recess at the extreme end of the airfield, that spotting was made impossible

Whilst the three Gladiators at Combolcia were readied in case the Italian fighters followed the SAAF bombers back to base, one Junkers 86 was hit by anti-aircraft fire overhead Gondar, and force-landed three miles from Bandina (Lieutenant Abbot, plus his crew of five). Dad managed to get in one, fairly lengthy operational sortie, albeit that two thirds was flown in total cloud. The next day, there was 8/8ths cloud over Gondar, grounding air operations. On 17th July, No 16 Squadron pilots had their first brush with the two CR 42 Fiats - their Hartbees were hit five times.

Dad also managed another two operational sorties on 25th and 27th July. The month was eventful, four significant sorties totalling two and a quarter hours flown. Captain Lucas certified Dads logbook. Meanwhile, Sir Pierre van Ryneveld was under pressure by the Air Ministry to deploy SAAF units to Egypt, and was becoming frustrated by General Nasi's defences at Gondar.

Gondar Castle

Italian General Nasi's stronghold – Gondar Castle

Alomata (1 August to 16 October 1941)

The three Gladiators of No 3 Squadron positioned at Alomata on the 1st August - arriving at 11h40, and flying on instruments for ten minutes to get through the cloud cover. The airstrip was less hazardous than Combolcia, but was still at an altitude of 5,000 feet. But then, it was only 140 miles east of Gondar. Dad is on the extreme right in the photo below.

August 1941 - what a month. A feast of flying at last, but not without its tragedies as well. August was the beginning of heavy SAAF loses at Gondar. Credit also needs to be given to the Italians for the exceptionally good ground defences. To list but a few highlights: 23 solo sorties. Nearly twenty eight hours flying; offensive operations into Eritrea, detachment to Alomata (Gondar) including a 19 day stint at forward base Alomata Satellite. Plus interception of Italian warplane *Savoia 79*, first solo on type Wapiti, a 643 percent increase in actual cloud instrument flying from 02·20 hours to 16·35 hours, and a cherry to top it off - the first birthday of Johannes Albertus Geldenhuys back in Johannesburg on the 15th.

By 4th August 1941, Lieutenant Colonel Bob Preller had assembled the depleted strength of four squadrons at Alomata for the attacks on Gondar. No 2 Wing had only the day before come under operational control of No 203 Group, RAF Asmara. With the Wing readied at Alomata Colonel Bob Preller was able to muster Nos 3, 15, 16 and 41 Squadrons against Gondar. The number of squadrons bore little relation to strength. In fact, No 3 Squadron had three Gladiators and two Hurricanes; No 15 Squadron was reduced to two Battles; No 16 Squadron had three Ju 86s; No 41 Squadron was best off with 18 of the indestructible Hartbees. A total of 28 aircraft at full serviceability.

On the 4th August Colonel Preller informed Air Headquarters East Africa and No 203 Group that a maximum effort against Gondar had begun that morning. In the next three days 46 sorties were made with machine-guns and bombs. Heavy anti-aircraft fire was met on every occasion. The bombardment was pursued with an intensity that kept aircraft over the enemy virtually every day of August. It was carried out with a disregard for the condition of the aircraft and terrain, which cost the SAAF its heaviest aircraft losses of the entire East African campaign. In August alone, Italian anti-aircraft defences, well protected in caves, shot down six Hartbees, three Gladiators and a Hurricane; several Junkers were rendered unserviceable. Pilots made hazardous emergency landings and some marched over 100 miles to safety.

A *Chicago News* war correspondent described the terrain between Alomata airfield and Gondar thus: "The stupendous canyon country of northern Abyssinia above Lake Tana -- from the open cockpit savage chasms stretch in every direction -- maps around Gondar leave contour lines unfinished". And from a pilots diary "The most rugged country I have seen in Africa -- peak upon peak, with deep ravines -- villages perched crazily on the brink of gorges".

On the first days of the operations against Gondar's anti-aircraft posts, other pilots had rude experiences with the difficult terrain. A Gladiator was badly damaged and a Hartbees piloted by Lieutenant Rothman came down out of fuel and was wrecked; the pilot escaped unhurt and made his way to Alomata on foot. To Captain Peter Hayden-Thomas (Dads first Flight Commander), fell a remarkable adventure. His Hurricane was hit by flak at Azozo airfield. Half-blinded and choked by fumes and smoke from the engine, he flew for 25 miles before making a high-speed pancake landing. Almost at once firing broke out. He had landed within 200 metres of an Italian fort. With the aid of friendly natives he ran for it, followed for an hour by Italians, firing continuously. For the next seven days he travelled on mule back along narrow, winding mountain trails, deviating every few miles to avoid Italian outposts. He made a journey of over 80 miles with Ethiopian soldiers trotting beside him. When he arrived at Debra Tabor, then in patriot hands, a runner was sent 90 miles across the mountains to inform No 3 Squadron.

Still on the 4th August, Dad flew at last light to a Satellite landing ground. Then at first light on the 6th, he returned to Alomata for a TOT (time over target) at Gondar timed for

08h00. On this particular operational sortie, he actually doubled his total cloud instrument flying. That is, two hours ten, out of two hours thirty. In other words, he only had 'visual' flight for a grand total of 20 minutes, which includes TOT, take-off and landing. The second sortie was not much better. After a very long day, he once again returned to the Satellite landing ground at last light. After a total of five hours ten (three forty-five spent in cloud) for the day, I can just imagine him collapsing on his fartsack (excuse the French), too tired to get drunk in the pub - although I would doubt whether one existed at the Satellite, designed to disperse aircraft from attack.

A Hartbees with Second Lieutenant Anderson and Air Sergeant Bernstein was located near Dich in a badly damaged condition. They had failed to return from their operation the previous day. Despite the terrain, the crew escaped injury. Food, water and blankets were dropped with instructions to make a landing ground for a rescue attempt.

The 9th August was another very long day for Preller Geldenhuys. Take-off was at 05h55 for a dawn operational sortie at Gondar which lasted for three hours - the longest to date so far in the Gladiator - of which an hour twenty was in cloud (flying solely on instruments). A mid-morning positional flight from the satellite landing ground was carried out, followed by a dusk sortie, because in the afternoon Brigands had attacked Alomata airfield. A batman was shot whilst OC 41 Squadron was bathing in a stream. Later in the day, an officer of the escort for evacuees was killed and his body mutilated.

The 12th August was also eventful. Dad flew to Dabat and Debarech to attack Italian strongholds. Lieutenant Cobbeldick wrecked his Hurricane on the runway - thus accounting for the last Hurricane of No 3 Sqn. Dad actually got his bum off the ground five times that day - no doubt attributed to the sniper fire which Alomata was being subjected to. A Junkers 86 was written off on the runway when its undercarriage collapsed. On the 14th August WO II ACF Preller Geldenhuys, in a Gladiator, together with three Hartbees, went out to raid Debarech. Captain W Chapman and Air Sergeant W Bergman failed to return. Lieutenant G R Andrew, last seen over the target, was found the next day with his observer Air Sergeant Wahl.

Captain Chapman's Hartbees overturned while attempting a forced landing in wild, rugged country infested by brigands and lawless bands. The two men set fire to the aircraft and were watching it burn when shots rang out. From behind a tree the airmen tried to identify themselves, but firing went on. Air Sergeant Bergman, burned on one hand by acid from the batteries, was wounded in the other. Taken captive, they were manhandled and robbed. Next day a Battle piloted by Lieutenant Wildsmith of No 15 Squadron flew blankets and supplies to the crash only to find the aircraft burnt out. The worst was feared. By that time the two airmen were journeying on mule back, heavily guarded. They were taken 80 miles in five days, in pelting rain, to the camp of Fiterari Abebe at Derasghie, a chieftain co-operating with Major Ringrose's patriotic force. Here they were offered the use of the chief's razor, courteously treated and shortly afterwards returned to their squadron.

Dad could so easily have been one of his mates on that ill-fated raid on Debarech. He certainly escaped their fate by the skin of his teeth. Despite these unusual dangers and the loss of aircraft there was no slackening in the attacks against all defended localities. August 15th, a day of pelting rain and overcast skies. Also, the first birthday of Johannes Albertus Geldenhuys. What does it feel like to be a father for the first time, separated by the war from your spouse, being a hemisphere apart, not having seen your wife for the past four months and not knowing whether you would ever set eyes on your first born son. In view of all the losses, the thought must have crossed Dad's mind.

On the 18th August a Hartbees from Alomata failed to return. Captain Gouws force landed with engine trouble on amber, or tableland, only 200 yards short of a 500-foot precipice. A Captain du Toit found him the next day.

On the 19th August, Dad was tasked to take one of the four remaining Gladiators, No 1342, to Addis Ababa for urgent repairs. The Gladiator could not be fixed, necessitating an overnight stay. At 14h25 in the afternoon, he carried out a twenty-minute airtest, followed by final adjustments before departing just before four in the late afternoon for the two hour ten minute flight back to the Alomata Satellite landing ground - with more than half of the sortie, once again being flown in 8/8th cloud. Little did Dad realise the fate that awaited his Gladiator a mere five days hence.

Satellite Base Camp Site – and Dad with Pet Flight Mascot Baboon

Preparing the 'LG – Landing Ground

The 19th was also significant in that that was the day that Lieutenant Colonel Bob R H Preller handed over command of No 2 Wing to Lieutenant Colonel M C P Mostert, leaving Alomata for Nairobi. The day Mostert took command, the sole remaining Battle of No 15 Squadron made its last sortie and the unit was withdrawn to Kenya for re-equipment. No 16 Squadron, with four serviceable Junkers, was so reduced, that by 22nd August it ceased to operate on a squadron basis and became No 35 Flight. No 3 Fighter Squadron was also due for re-equipment on Mohawks a couple of days later - only to be accelerated by events that were still to unfold.

To all Ethiopian Officers and People:

Peace be to you.

The bearer of this letter is an Officer of the English Government and has come to help you and is a friend of Ethiopia. Treat him well; guard him from harm; give him food and drink, and help him to get to the nearest English soldiers, and you will be rewarded.

Words to be called out as soon as possible to establish identity—

Ingleez; Wadaj.

English; Friend.

It is advisable to approach unarmed if the situation permits.

Ethiopian, Somali and Borana letters issued to pilots, in the event of going down in enemy territory

On the 22nd August, eighteen days after Captain Peter Hayden-Thomas was shot down, he was rescued. The heavily bearded No 3 Squadron pilot called the affair "a grand experience." I bet Dad was pleased to welcome back his first operational flight commander who had given him his briefing.

On the 24th August, Dad was scrambled, in Gladiator number 1343, to identify an enemy Savoia 79 Italian bomber. The aircraft is a three-engine monoplane, with a crew of 4 to 5, a 2,750 bomb load, and armed with 3 x 12·7mm and 2 x 7·7mm cannons. This was certainly a formidable adversary for a mere single-seat Gloster fighter, armed with ·303s. Italian General Nasi had petitioned the Supreme Air Command for an S.79 on August the 8th, but General Santoro was reluctant to risk his dwindling air resources. As recently as April, the Regia Aeronautica was known to be operating at least three of these potent bombers.

On the 25th August Dad once again flew the two and a half-hour flight to Addis Ababa for aircraft modification to Gladiator No 1346. This time it took longer, and Dad had no alternative to wait the five days it took to carry out the engine test. The previous Gladiator that he brought came to grief the day he took off from Alomata. Was it fate? The reader may recall that No 3 Squadron was down to four Gladiators. Anyway, on that same day, Lieutenant W Arbuthnot, in Gladiator 1342, failed to return from an offensive reconnaissance of Azozo - and the following day, 26th August, Gladiator 1343, piloted by Lieutenant Mitchell was reported missing after an operation in the same area. The latter Gladiator was the same aircraft Dad had used to identify the Italian bomber, only the day before. Interesting, isn't it? Or perhaps, it was pure co-incidence.

Lieutenant Mitchell had an extraordinary escape. Realising that he had no choice but to crash-land he was forced to choose the ledge of a mountain. It was narrow and only about 50 yards long. "As I landed", he recalled (in a broadcast made in Nairobi) "the aircraft was cut in half. The tail fell down the mountain slope. The cockpit with me inside it remained on the ledge." He recovered consciousness with his head on an Abyssinians lap.

On the 29th Dad carried out a 20-minute engine air test, but I presume all was not well. Because just before midday the following day, he experienced what I would consider a very hairy first solo flight back to Alomata in a Westland Wapiti, No P624. Dad took off from Addis Ababa at 11h25, and set course northwards for Alomata. He now found himself, in an unfamiliar aircraft for the first time, in cloud, a very long two hours ten on instruments, and to touch down on terra firma three hours five after take-off. I can only presume that there were times that he was uncertain of his position (a navigator's term for being 'lost'), that he experienced dreadful vertigo - with such a long period in cloud, and was indeed fortunate to arrive at his destination in one piece. I call that courage of the highest order.

The effect of the accumulated aircraft losses since the beginning of the Gondar offensive was regarded as grave. Air Headquarters sent a signal to the Officer Commanding No 2 Wing on the 28th August pointing out the heavy losses in his squadrons over the past three weeks - seven out of nine due to anti-aircraft fire. Air Commodore Sowrey considered that present operations did not warrant risks through pressing home attacks at low level. He urged more control over the squadrons.

Captain G Lucas, Officer Commanding, 'B' Flight, No 3 Squadron, certified WO II Preller Geldenhuys's logbook as having flown 27·50 hours for the month, of which 14·25 was operational: Gladiator, 14·15 instrument/cloud flying, and 3·05 first solo Wapiti. Dad had been through the 'wars' with a mere grand total 211·40 hours - and had lived to record his contribution.

Lieutenant Colonel Mostert was ordered to reduce daily attacks and conserve resources for the main offensive now postponed until November when dry weather would increase its chances of success. Three days later Hartbees attacked the Italian Colonial Brigade at Minzero. Impetuous young airmen continued to attack with as much ardour as before. Four more Hartbees and a Junkers 86 was lost before Air Commodore Sowrey again protested in a signal on 17 September that air losses were very perturbing. Lieutenant Colonel Mossie Mostert replied that operations were being carried out under difficult conditions with obsolete aircraft and inexperienced pilots. Meanwhile, the Mohawks had been a great disappointment to the SAAF. A serious defect was revealed in the Mohawk engine. This meant that No 2 Squadron, stripped of all its aircraft to keep Nos 1 and 3 Squadrons going, could not be re-equipped as planned.

On 12th September, Dad flew a short 20-minute sortie to identify a Gladiator. His allocated aircraft was No 1339, an older machine, which shortly thereafter required an engine airtest.

Wolchefit appeared to offer an insurmountable obstacle on the way to Gondar. The continuing rains (which Dad could testify to) had made the advance from Dessie through Debra Tabor impossible. At this stage changes came about in East Africa Command and bringing what remained of the RAF in Eritrea under direct control of No 2 Wing SAAF at Alomata.

On 15th September 1941, Lieutenant General Sir William Platt was given the new East Africa Command with headquarters at Nairobi. On 20th September General Platt arrived at Alomata by air from Addis Ababa with General Wetherall and General Fowkes to consider plans for finishing off the East African campaign. The following day, Lieutenant Colonel

Mostert left Alomata for Asmara to attend a conference about the coming operations. With all that 'Brass' mingling at Alomata, I suspect Dad, although scarce, would most likely have been kept well informed. I bet he was itching to get going again. He did not have long to wait. Events started happening.

On 29th September, Warrant Officer II Preller Geldenhuys carried out an armed reconnaissance mission to Feroaber, opposite Lake Tana, and on the track between Ifag and Minzera. The weather conditions were improving. Although still well defended, the Italians were engaging in acts of sabotage and paid little heed to events at Wolchefit. Dad also dropped pamphlets in Italian and Amharic (the local dialect).

Two days earlier, Colonel Gonella in command of the garrison at Wolchefit, made a decision unexpected by General Platt. He surrendered. The Italians were well dug in, in their deep, 30-foot tunnels and caves. They had been the target of continuous air attack, as well as subjected to the hell of artillery fire. The official Italian account of the campaign gives casualties at Wolchefit as 950 killed and wounded. Colonel Gonella surrendered with 1,631 Italians and 1,450 Colonial troops. The day before the Italians marched down the pass - so badly damaged that it would take a fortnight to clear the road - a Hartbees dropped a message to advancing troops to advise them that negotiations for an armistice were in progress.

In the period 4th August to 10th October, Gondar suffered the assault of 96,000lbs of bombs (43 tons) and 74,450 rounds. The remaining garrisons of the defended areas could not be attacked with confidence until the end of the rains, in November, when it was planned for the main force to concentrate at Amba Giorgis on the road from the north, while a column attacked the Kulkaber-Feroaber position from the direction of Dessie. Gondar was in fact to be attacked from all sides. As part of the closing in on the final areas of resistance, the detachment of No 3 Squadron and part of No 41 Squadron began to move to Dabat. Dabat was on the road south towards Gondar, in the area made safe by the fall of Wolchefit, and well placed to be used in the final attack on Gondar.

Dabat

Warrant Officer II Preller Geldenhuys positioned Dabat, in Gladiator No 1344, shortly after eight in the morning of 16th October, having taken off from Alomata over an hour earlier. This was the same Gladiator that he had used to attack Feroaber at the end of September. Fate would treat him kindly, with No 1344 being his preferred choice, despite the earlier demises of Nos 1343 and 1342. At four o'clock in the afternoon, Dad took off again for a lengthy one hour thirty-five reconnaissance sortie to Azozo - a target he would attack another three times. On the 17th, Dad carried out an operational reconnaissance sortie against Ambazzo, just north of, and defending Gondar from a northerly assault. But now back to Paddy Hope, Dad's flying instructor, and also the disposition of the SAAF units.

The disposition of No 2 Wing in October was as follows. At Dabat, Advanced No Wing; 'B' Flight No 3 Squadron (3 Gladiators - Major Lucas, Lieutenant Hope and Dad), "C" Flight No 41 Squadron. At Alomata, HQ No 2 Wing and "A" Flight No 3 Squadron, "B" Flight, No 41 Squadron. At Addis Ababa, HQ No 41 Squadron. The Junkers 86s of No 35 Flight had by this time been transferred to Aiscia.

That the Italians realised Dabat was well placed to support the final attack and to increase the miseries of those under siege may be seen in the fact that the ground party had no sooner arrived at the new landing ground, when an aircraft (which might have been a Gladiator) made a close approach and opened fire. It was a Fiat CR 42 from Azozo, flown most probably by Italian pilot 2nd Lieutenant Ildebrando Malavolti. But it caused no casualties. Dad and the rest of the airmen settled in - and pilots made many flights against the bold Italian - without success.

It was bitterly cold after sundown on the 8,500-foot plateau. The airmen wore greatcoats, sweaters and mufflers, slept under many blankets but could not keep warm in the cold rarefied air. With typical adaptability under hard conditions they made armchairs out of petrol-boxes and fashioned windbreaks out of empty petrol tins. Messes were brightened with flowers stuck in empty beer bottles.

On 24th October Gladiator pilot Preller Geldenhuys "silenced one ack-ack nest" at Ambazzo. The day before, a successful raid had been carried out against Celga, situated to the west of Azozo, as well as on Gondar itself. This was Dad's first attack on Celga, but now his third on Gondar itself. Another three were to take place.

At 17h35, Dad, together with his training instructor, Paddy Hope were scrambled as the result of an aircraft flying southwards at about 2,000 feet over Dabat. Its flight was concealed in low cloud. A few seconds later the Fiat CR 42 was seen through a gap. Whilst Dad provided aerodrome top cover, Paddy Hope sighted the quarry and pursued it southwards through gaps in the cloud. Over Ambazzo he found it circling about 1,000 feet below and dived after him. The Italian pilot took violent evasive action as the South African's guns opened fire and he made a climbing turn into the setting sun. Lieutenant Hope followed his every move pouring fire into the aircraft as it hung poised at the top of its climb. As it began its spiral to the fields below the Gladiator got in a final short burst. A flicker of flame came from the Fiat; it spun into the ground and turned on to its back. Lieutenant Paddy Hope circled the funeral pyre of the last Italian airman to be killed in combat in the Abyssinia campaign. The flight had lasted barely two minutes and had ended, almost symbolically, as the sun set among the great cold peaks. It was a good day for No 3 Squadron. Dad had silenced an anti-aircraft gun that morning at Ambazzo, and was airborne with the dusk scramble when Gloster Gladiators shot the last Italian fighter out the skies. I might add - Dad recorded a full 20 minutes cloud flying for his twenty-minute mission.

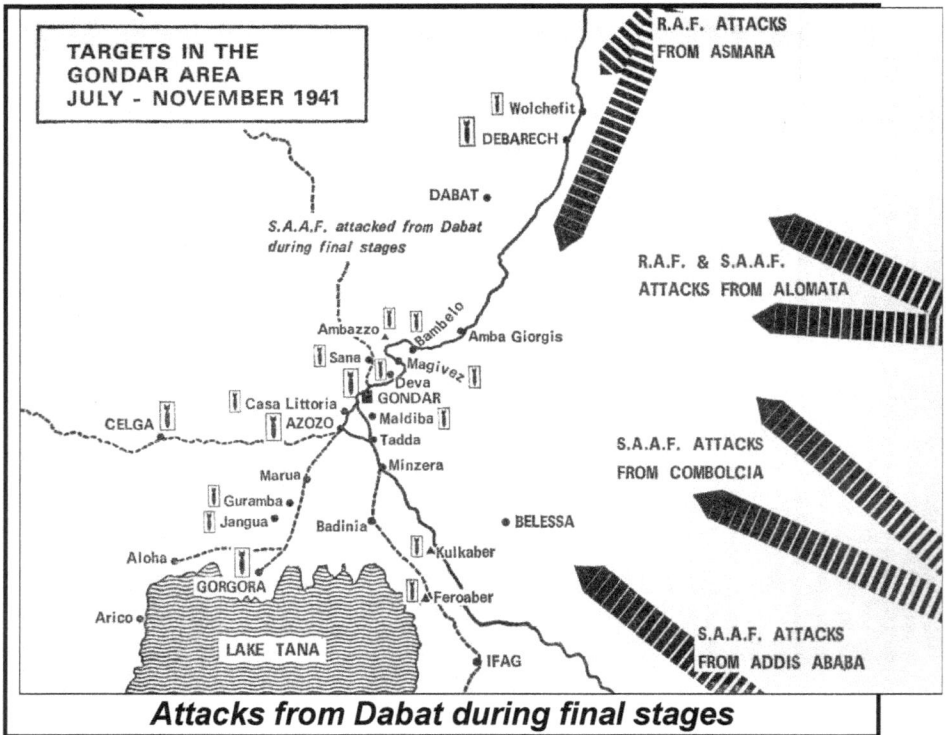

TARGETS IN THE GONDAR AREA JULY - NOVEMBER 1941

R.A.F. ATTACKS FROM ASMARA

Wolchefit

DEBARECH

DABAT

S.A.A.F. attacked from Dabat during final stages

R.A.F. & S.A.A.F. ATTACKS FROM ALOMATA

Ambazzo

Bambelo

Amba Giorgis

Sana

Magivez

Deva

GONDAR

Casa Littoria

CELGA

AZOZO

Maldiba

Tadda

Minzera

S.A.A.F. ATTACKS FROM COMBOLCIA

Marua

Guramba

Jangua

Badinia

BELESSA

Aloha

Kulkaber

GORGORA

Feroaber

Arico

LAKE TANA

IFAG

S.A.A.F. ATTACKS FROM ADDIS ABABA

Attacks from Dabat during final stages

Aircraft crash in East Africa

The next day, 25th October a ground party, sent from Dabat, found the remains of the aircraft about 30 yards east of the Gondar road - the charred body still in the cockpit. The pilot's skull was broken and there were four bullet holes in the back of the seat. The South Africans were amazed to find that the condition of the unburned fabric was superior to that on their own aircraft. The CR 42 was fitted with wireless, its ammunition bore the mark 1941 and it had eleven fresh patches, presumed from hits received when it attacked the ground party at Dabat on 15th October. The following day, the 26th, Dad flew a reconnaissance/top cover sortie to Ambazzo. The South African airmen were touched by the death of this lone pilot. Paddy Hope dropped a farewell tribute on Ambazzo.

Colonel Busoni radioed the following message to Rome. "Tribute to pilot of Fiat. He was a brave one - South African Air Force." Arrangements were made for an Italian priest to come from a regiment below the Gondar escarpment and give the remains a Christian burial.

Three days later Paddy Hope was shot down. At that time the Italians were using motorboats on Lake Tana, bringing in supplies by night at Gorgora. Many bombing and machine-gunning sorties were made against the jetties there. Lieutenant Hope planned to attack the transport columns carrying supplies up to Gondar by moonlight. The flight, after dark on 31st October, was made on his own initiative. Lieutenant Hope, according to current reports, was a convinced believer in astrology, and found the astral portents to be propitious for his dangerous and unauthorised venture. As expected, he found a convoy on its way up the precipitous road from the lake and attacked. The Italians fought back and the Gladiator was set on fire. Lieutenant Hope crash-landed in the darkness in the burning machine. The first indication of his fate came from a Rome Radio announcement.

Ten days later a man of the Habash tribe - used by the Italians to smuggle messages from Gondar to Asmara - brought a note to Dabat. Written in pencil on Ala Littoria notepaper, it was addressed to Captain Shuttleworth: "Dear Skipper, God knows if this will reach you. I was hit by a bullet in the petrol tank. The aircraft caught fire and I had to crash-land at 200 mph. It hit a tree, bounced up, slow rolled and crashed right side up, the cockpit was a mass of flames. I got out somehow, face severely burnt, all my hair burnt off. Then I was shot in the head by an excited askari and whacked with a rifle butt before being rescued by two Italian officers. A doctor fixed me up. That night I went blind and for two days and nights it was awful. I can see now but will be in hospital at least 15 days." He asked for cigarettes, shaving kit, toothbrush and an Italian-English dictionary. "P.S. The medical people are very decent to me."

In 1940 he was one of the few who participated in the East African campaign against Italy as a pilot in the South African Air Force.

WW2 Hawker Hartebeest combat pilot in East Africa tells his story: Lawrie Shuttleworth

Captain, later Lt Col Lawrie Shuttleworth

In the exchange of civilised courtesies that followed, toilet articles were dropped by a home-made parachute on Azozo, Gondar's airfield. On the safe return of Lieutenant Paddy Hope to No 3 Squadron an inquiry was conducted on 30th November by Lieutenant Colonel M C P Mostert. The court martial found that Lieutenant Hope's act had been actuated by excessive zeal and over-keenness.

It is also worth mentioning that Dad was the one that was sent on 1st November duty, and I quote "Gondar - Gorgora. Search for missing Glad. Bullet glanced off tank." Research also revealed, and I quote 'On 1st November, a Gladiator and a Hartbees found a large barge and a number of pleasure vessels at Gorgora and fired 1,500 rounds at the boats.' I can only presume that he counted his lucky stars, and escaped by the skin of his teeth - again. It was a bullet that hit Paddy Hope's petrol tank and set the aircraft on fire. In addition, Dad's sortie was flown in broad daylight - from 10h25 to

12h30, versus the cover of darkness the night before, for Paddy Hope. But then, on the other hand, just consider the hazards of carrying out ground attacks at night, as well as the terrain between Gorgora and Gondar. Now, many years later, I can kick myself for not confirming my findings first hand - whilst Dad was still alive.

Also of interest, is the sortie flown by Dad for the remaining Fiat hunt at Azozo on 29th October, and providing fighter escort to a Wellesley on a photographic mission the next day.

November was the most eventful month of the Abyssinia campaign that was fast drawing to a close. Just after the narrow escape, a crippled Hartbees limped back to Dabat and Dad was scrambled to indicate the direction of landing to the Hartbees.

On the fifth, two sorties were carried out tasked with conducting Fiat hunts. The first was of a brief fifteen minutes duration, but the second entailed a dogfight over Azozo during a fifty-five minute sortie. I recall, as a starry-eyed school kid, being fascinated by Dogfight Dixon's escapades in the comic strips - his technique on being bounced was to execute a half-roll, pull through a loop and follow it by a roll off the top and thereby bring his own gun-sights to bear on the Hun. No way, my father assured me. No matter how alert you think you are, whenever you are caught unawares by an attacker diving at you from out the sun, or as soon as enemy fire starts whistling past you, all hell breaks loose. Pandemonium reigns with a kicking and a gouging in the cockpit. Rudder pedals are kicked from one side to the other, simultaneously pulling, pushing and applying full aileron in rolling manoeuvres while the adrenaline rushes through the body. No sooner do you come to your senses than you find you are alone in an empty sky, with nobody in sight, be they friend or foe. Apprehensively you make your way back to base, only to find that you are not alone. Half the formation have already landed, the remainder returning in dribs and drabs, and the unfortunates not returning at all, either being posted "missing", or "killed in action". For those with confirmed kills, spirits would be sky high, morale high, and much telling of war stories. It was a message I remembered well, together with my father's sound advice of "There are old pilots, and there are bold pilots - but there are few old bold pilots." It wouldn't surprise me if he coined the phrase after his many narrow escapes, and with hindsight.

It should be remembered that the Italians enjoyed superior numbers - that they had better equipment, and that fighting in Abyssinia during the 1935-1936 period gave the Italian Air Force actual combat experience before World War II broke out in September 1939 - or the Italians declaring war in June 1940. In any event - back to the happenings of November 1941.

On 8th November, Dad was given the task of escorting and protecting three Wellesleys to Gondar on a bombing and pamphlet dropping mission. The next day Dad was scrambled on a similar mission, but this time for the 'identification of aircraft - three Wellesleys and Gladiator returning from a raid'.

WELLESLEY   47 SQDN

Meanwhile forces were gathering for the final assault on Gondar, for despite the fall of its outposts and the continual harassment of the defences, General Nasi's determination to hold out to the last made necessary the planning of a considerable operation. The abrupt collapse of the defenders of Wolchefit had given rise to the optimistic assumption that the great rock bulwark in the south, at Kulkaber, would collapse as quickly. Such was not to be the case. From the air, Kulkaber Pass had the appearance of a faint scar on an impenetrable face of rock; among its approaches and cliffs. The soldiers and artillery of Colonel Ugolini looked southwards, knowing that the enemy must come from this direction. He did not intend to give in easily and it soon became evident that it would be a well-planned operation to dislodge him from his eyrie.

At this stage it might be helpful to re-visualise the area of Gondar. The town itself was still the centre of resistance of a defended area a hundred miles in diameter, framed on three sides by massive ranges and on the fourth by Lake Tana. Every road to Gondar had formidable natural defences, which the Italians had supplemented by entrenchments. Within the circle of outer defences were numerous defended areas and forts built in all but inaccessible positions, extensive minefields and well-concealed artillery. Fortress Gondar was, Major General Fowkes commented after its fall, "a tough nut to crack".

Available to the SAAF for the coming operations were a total of forty-five aircraft, based at Dabat and Alomata; among them were fifteen new, fast, bomb carrying Curtiss P 36 Mohawks of No 3 Squadron. By now, the engineers had sorted out the previous problems with their Wright Cyclone engines. As a JP, Dad would have to wait awhile before carrying out the conversion to type. Anyway, the Mohawks boobed on their first sortie on the 9th - they attacked their own troops, killing three and wounding sixteen soldiers of the 12th Division.

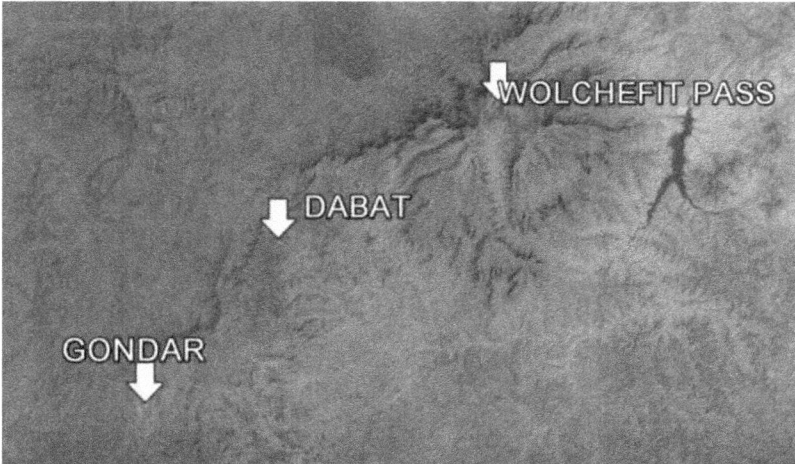

On 11th November, a large air operation sent thirty sorties against Ambazzo, Celga, Deva, Gorgora and Jangua on the road to Gondar from the lake - where large concentrations had been noted. On the 11th Dads mission was to escort Lieutenant Colonel Ormsby in a Hartbees over the enemy front line positions during a sortie of 1.20-hour duration. Ormsby's task was to spot the main gun positions and likely emplacements at Gondar. A few days later he was dead - killed in a foray by an Italian Fiat aircraft.

On 12th November aircraft carried out heavy attacks south of Feroaber in preparation for an attack by infantry. Two fell victim to Italian fire. Second Lieutenant G van Dyk (with Sergeant Keeton) was seen to break formation and head for Dabat. He had shot away a portion of the cooling system with his own front guns. Lieutenant A W Penver and Air Sergeant Viljoen force landed 70 miles east of Gondar in a position that could not be reached by road or track. The stranded airmen organised villagers to stamp down an airstrip. Three days later, Dad was required to escort a Hartbees in his trusty Gladiator No 1344 to the scene of the forced landing in enemy territory (to drop messages regarding rescue plans), and then to proceed on to Minzero and Azozo. However, the three hour sortie was not without its own problems which necessitated a short air test after the adjustment was made to the pitch of the airscrew - entailing a climb to 10,000 feet and checking airspeed at 175 mph.

On 13th November, OC 47 Squadron RAF, Squadron Leader Illsley and his observer, Sergeant Rann, were killed when a Wellesley engine seized through an oil-pipe breaking. As he tried to force-land on a hill, the aircraft stalled and spun in. On 14th November Hartbeests were over Kulkaber, and the next day, over Celga, the escarpment to the west. On both occasions they met with concentrated ground fire. During bombing, Captain W Chapman's aircraft was hit by a bullet that severed the bomb release connection forcing him to make three violent dives in order to release the bombs hung up.

On 20th November Dad was required to carry out two sorties to 2nd Lieutenant Penver and Air Sergeant Viljoen to inspect the 250 x 30 yards runway near Metsefet where the aircrew had force landed. And the next day took off again in his Gladiator to drop supplies to the unfortunate airman. Thirteen days after their ordeal, on 25th November, they flew out in time for the last assault on Gondar. I bet Penver and Dad must have enjoyed a couple of beers in the pub when they were re-united.

On 22nd November, the Italian Fiat CR 42 was taken from its hiding-place in a cave at Azozo and made an attack on the British artillery at Kulkaber, killing Lieutenant Colonel Ormsby with the single burst it fired. The Fiat returned to Azozo and was once more hidden. It will be recalled that Dad had provided fighter escort to Ormsby on the 11th, The good news was that the Regia Aeronautica days in East Africa were numbered.

On 26th November, Dad's Gladiator provided fighter escort and protection for 2nd Lieutenant Anderson flying a Hartbeest on a reconnaissance and bombing raid on the Ambazzo to Gondar road. I suspect Anderson (with his observer Bernstein) was somewhat apprehensive following his August

4th forced landing near Ditch when his Hartbeest was badly damaged. He was no doubt consoled having Gladiator pilot Geldenhuys providing the comforting fighter escort. Whilst this mission was in progress, air force officers were at a conference to discuss the big attack scheduled for the next day, when a report came in that the hanger at Azozo aerodrome was burning furiously. Within it, the last Fiat CR 42 of the Regina Aeronautica had been reduced to a charred skeleton by its last pilot. Meanwhile, artillery and aircraft continuously attacked targets about the town.

On 27th November morning of the final assault, as the aircraft were being started up on Dabat's airfield and gunners were climbing into rear cockpits, a pilot of No 41 Squadron noted that the infantry were "going in today". The day they had been waiting for so long seemed at last to have come. Eight Mohawks of No 3 Squadron, six Wellesleys and sixteen Hartbees were to take part in the final attack. That the town would fall, despite its vast superiority in numbers, was inevitable. How many would die in the next twenty-four hours was the question - for inner Gondar could be defended from many well-armed points of resistance.

Half an hour before dawn a terrific artillery barrage lit the hills and the infantry began to go forward. The first aircraft took off. In the next few hours they were to drop 12,544 lbs of bombs.

The 26th East African Brigade attacked the Defeccia Ridge, while the 25th East Africa Brigade advanced up the main road to Azozo, and Major Douglas attacked the positions known as the Fanta Pass. As the attackers came closer to the town the din of continual explosions and the crackle of small-arms fire were increased by the defenders' destruction of ammunition dumps and magazines. The armoured cars had hardly cleared Azozo airfield when a Hartbeest, its engine badly hit by anti-aircraft fire, made the first landing of a SAAF aircraft at Gondar. Second Lieutenant Robinson was uninjured, and his gunner Sergeant Louw (the diarist laughingly recorded), would be eating off the mantelpiece for a few days. In one of the hangars still-warm cups of coffee were discovered.

At 13h50 Battle Headquarters sent a message to No 2 Wing that demolitions were going on all around Gondar and requesting all available aircraft to be ready for bombing attacks which might be required to finish the enemy off. Resistance was particularly stubborn at the village of Deva, five miles from the centre of the town. A battery there, part of a very strongly defended position, defied both shells and bombs until the end. At main centres of resistance such as Torelli's Camp, Deva, Moldiba and Larei as many as ten Hartbeests kept up continuous attacks until white flags appeared, mushroom-like, as the diarist described it, among the enemy trenches.

It was about 15h00. Half an hour later General Nasi sent a message to Major-General Fowkes, asking his terms for an armistice. General Fowkes replied: "Unconditional surrender." The battle continued for another three hours, until with coming dusk the sound of rifle-fire and mortars were heard in the streets of the town. The Italian battery on Deva Hill continued in action until ordered to cease fire.

Italian Surrender - Gondar

Circling above the murk near sundown, two Hartbeests, Lieutenant Maree and 2nd Lieutenant Royce, saw the moment of Italian surrender and the fluttering of the first white flags at evening as General Nasi declared all resistance at an end.

Lieutenant Kenneth Andrews, as special air force correspondent, described the last moments of the last Italian citadel in the fallen empire: "Italian soldiers lined the roads, unshaven and dirty. They stood in the doorways of trenches tunnelled into the hills. Some stood sullenly, others smiling. Most of them carried rifles. Corpses lay on the roads. Over

Gondar lay a pall of smoke - its shops were closed, its windows barricaded. Overhead, Mohawks and Hartbeests patrolled. We drove to the Banca d'Italia. As we drew up, a white sheet was waved from the roof. Three of us were ushered through scores of Italians into the General's office. Slight, bespectacled, with bird-like features, General Nasi stood up and saluted". Lieutenant Andrews went up to the roof of a partially constructed three-story building and ran up the Union Jack. Overhead SAAF aircraft were diving and looping in the smoke of the fallen town.

The next day, messages written in the general's own hand, were dropped. The outlying garrisons at Gorgora and Celga were instructed to surrender. 11,500 Italians and 12,000 African troops went into captivity. Men of the SAAF who examined the badly damaged town with its intricate system of trenches, found much evidence of their own work. In the burnt-out hangar at Azozo were the charred remains of the last CR 42. The Italian airmen had hung buckets of petrol under the wings and propeller and so destroyed the last survivor of the mighty air fleet that had subdued Ethiopia in 1936.

Second Lieutenant Preller Geldenhuys still had one more sortie to do - which nearly turned to disaster. He took off in Gladiator No 1344 at 11h55 on 28th November on an aircraft test flight. Whilst gliding inverted, that is upside-down for the uninitiated, his Bristol Mercury engine cut out. He was now faced with no other choice but to go down with the aircraft on a forced landing. His logbook entry reads 'forced landed on 'drome'. I presume he made it back to Dabat, and wasn't beating up Gondar where the previous day SAAF aircraft were looping the loop. I also presume the observant reader would have noted that he had been promoted to commissioned rank - a just reward for his war contributions.

That same day, Lieutenant-General Wetherall, GOC (General Officer Commanding) East Africa, closed the record of fighting in Ethiopia in a final tribute addressed to the Air Officer Commanding, Air Commodore Sowrey. "I am now at Gondar," he wrote, "I hear on all sides of the splendid and gallant work carried out by the air forces - no task was too difficult, no day too long". Italian Fascism in East Africa had been destroyed. German Nazism was starting to crumble.

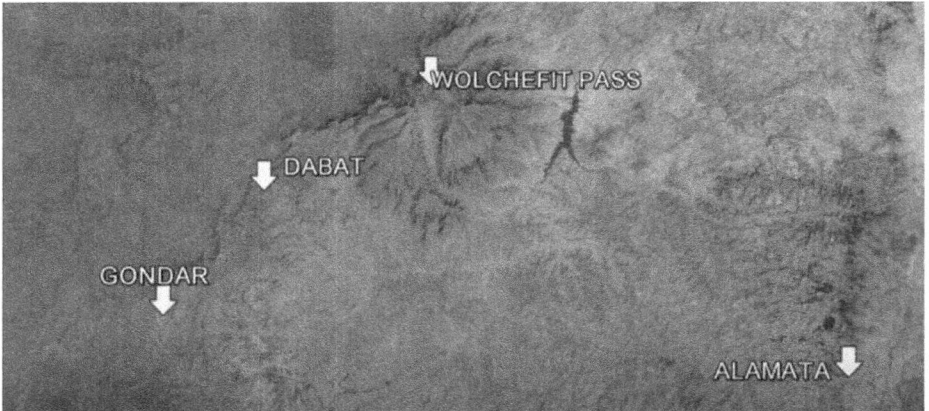

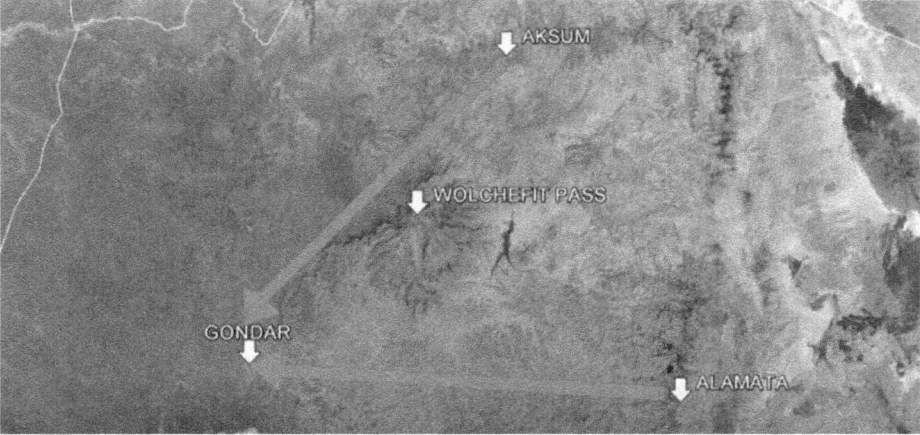

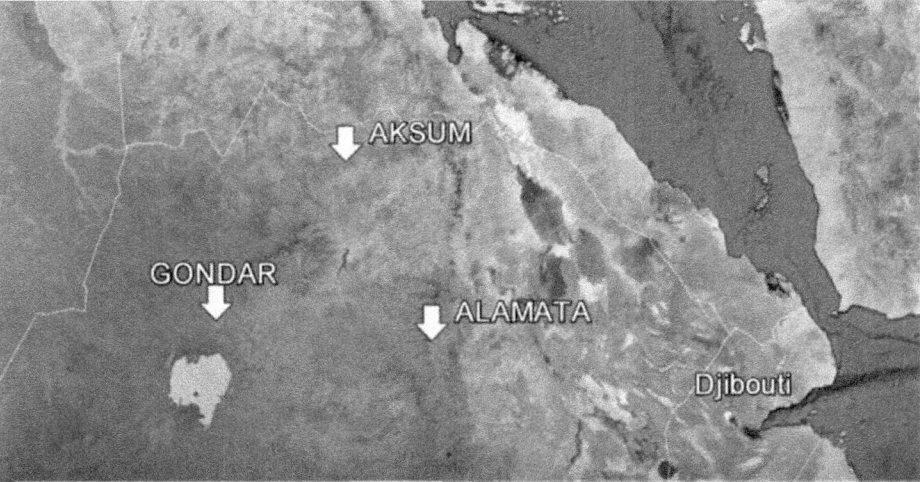

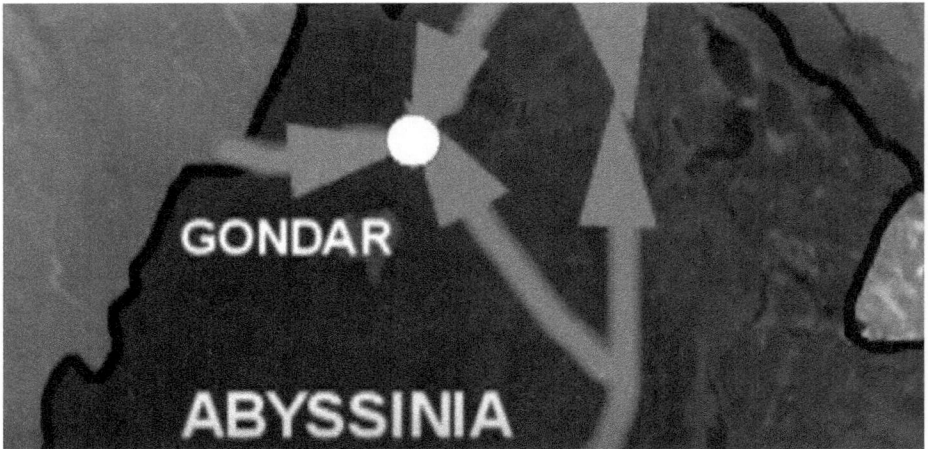

GONDAR

ABYSSINIA

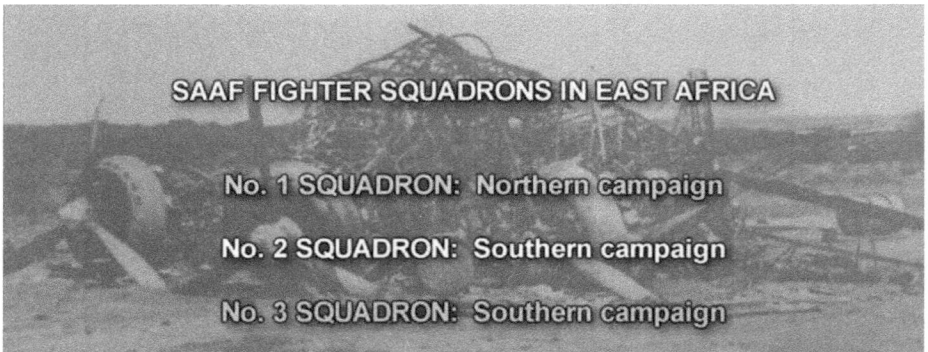

SAAF FIGHTER SQUADRONS IN EAST AFRICA

No. 1 SQUADRON: Northern campaign

No. 2 SQUADRON: Southern campaign

No. 3 SQUADRON: Southern campaign

Nos 1, 2 and 3 Squadrons in East Africa

Fiat CR-42
Speed: 441 Km/h
2 x 12,7 mm machine guns

Air War in East Africa 1940-1941 (South African Air Force perspective)

Note this video clip, screen-saved at 3:52, showing the family photo of ACFP Geldenhuys during the War in East Africa 1940 - 1941

No 3 Fighter Squadron - Recall

Major G W Lucas, OC 3 Squadron, briefed his surviving pilots that there was no time to lose. There was an urgent need to re-equip and re-deploy the SAAF squadrons for service elsewhere. Sir Pierre van Ryneveld was concerned with No 1 Squadron in Egyptian Middle East as well as pilot training by veterans in the Union for No 10 Fighter Squadron. Their immediate task was to deliver and hand over all serviceable aircraft. The end of November was party time, celebrating the end of the Abyssinian Campaign. The land forces battle casualties in East Africa and Abyssinia amounted to 270, of whom 73 had been killed.

On 1st December Dad departed Dabat for the last time with Gladiator No 1344, and set course for Alomata. The next day was a long day - take-off at 06h40 for Asmara, then on to Kassala, and on to Khartoum. Five minutes later, he was airborne again for Gordon's Tree, arriving there at 17h45 - having logged 6 hours 55 minutes flying time for the day. That is quite a lot for a fighter pilot - and also to areas which one is unfamiliar with. I bet a rather nostalgic farewell was bid to Gladiator 1344, one of the very few Gladiators to survive the ravages of air warfare.

Also, on 1st December, Lieutenant Colonel Bob R H Preller DFC resigned his commission. He seemed under great stress and pleaded the suicidal nature of tasks laid on the Maryland's of No 12 Squadron, flying without escorts into swarms of fighters. A crisis in squadron leadership ensued, affecting Nos 1, 2, 4, and 12 Squadron. A Captain Osler, Major Krummeck, Captain Kriel and Lieutenant Colonel Bosch were duly appointed on 5th December to command the respective squadrons.

On 4th December 1941 at 05h45, Dad boarded Short Sunderland "Corinthian", captained by Captain Finnegan, and set course for Malakan, then onto Juba, Port Bell and landing at Kisumu on the north-east shores of Lake Victoria at 17h20. Kisumu to Nairobi was either by road or rail for extensive debriefing sessions, over a period of one week.

Short Sunderland

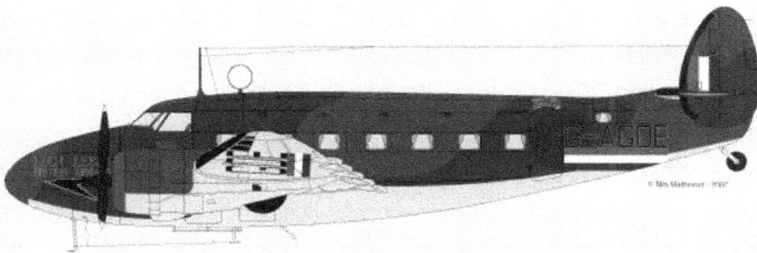
Lodestar

On 11th December Second Lieutenant Preller Geldenhuys boarded Lodestar 249, the 'Sir Henry Pottinger' at Nairobi for Dodoma (in Tanganyika), night stopping at Kasama in

Northern Rhodesia. Early next morning, course was set for Lusaka, Bulawayo, Zwartkop Air Station, landing Germiston at 15h00. I would speculate a great sigh of relief to arrive back in one piece, and not in a wooden box. A well-earned rest ensued, with the remnants of No 3 Squadron under Major G Lucas assembling at Zwartkop Air Station late February 1942.

On 27th February 1942, Dad required a mere 10 minute check-out with Captain Wildsmith in Harvard 1303, before he himself took the aircraft up for 35 minutes familiarisation. He had not forgotten Squadron Leader Gibb, CFI of No 20 SFTS Cranborne's instruction on the Harvard aircraft type of May the previous year. March entailed flying mainly Harvards (a picture of a SAAF Harvard is shown on the next page) and one second pilot photo sortie in twin engine Gloster, powered by two Bristol Jupiter engines.

On 24th April 1942, Second Lieutenant Preller Geldenhuys bade No 3 Squadron farewell and was posted to No 10 Fighter Squadron, based Durban, also equipped with Harvards. His first sortie with this squadron was on the 28th and two days later he flew with a Corporal Geldenhuys - a relative that is unknown at this time. On 6th May Dad flew with Lieutenant Paddy Hope in Harvard 1301 - I guess he would have been a Captain by now had it not been for his courts-martial in East Africa. However, L C H Hope would make good later, find fame and fortune in that that he shot down a Messerschmitt 109F whilst with No 2 Squadron at El Alamein, damaged another a month later, and when he was shot up on 11th November 1942. Paddy Hope had his hydraulic system shot away; oil covered the interior of his cockpit and obscured the windscreen. He could only see through a cannon shell hole but managed to get the Kittyhawk safely down. During early June, Dad also flew two 'wheel landing' sorties with Lieutenant Peak and 2nd Lieutenant Davidson - both pilots who were subsequently killed.

Now for some background. It will be remembered that Japan entered World War II when Japanese bombers destroyed the

United States Pacific Fleet at Pearl Harbour on 8th December 1941. Two days later, the *Prince of Wales* and *Repulse* were sunk off Kuantan by Japanese dive-bombers. These two battleships came to the Cape waters in November 1941, and were provided with continual Coastal Air Force (South African) air cover over them. On 25th December Hong Kong surrendered and the way was set for Japanese conquest. Soon they would make their first appearance in the Indian Ocean and Japanese aircraft would be heard over Durban. Intensified submarine warfare was now expected and, in view of the possibility of coastal ports being bombarded by battleships, the Chief of General Staff Field Marshal Jannie Smuts asked the British Air Ministry in January 1942 to supply long-range Beauforts. Two new coastal units were to be formed for the expected struggle. They were to be crack units with the best crews available. However, Japan had entered the war before the Beauforts were even shipped from England. So the year 1941 ended. By May 1942 Japanese submarines were appearing off Madagascar and sinking took place in the Moçambique Channel and in the approaches to Delagoa Bay. A Japanese raider-supply vessel sank a ship off the Zululand coast. It was the beginning of a bitter year in which war came in earnest to southern waters.

Five submarines and two supply ships of the 8th Submarine Flotilla commanded by Admiral Ishizaki carried out the Japanese offensive in the Indian Ocean. Two of the submarines carried aircraft and three carried midget submarines. The Admiral's flagship 1-10 was also equipped with a single-seater aircraft. They were responsible for torpedoing the *Ramillies* and the tanker *British Royalty*, and sinking the *Elysia*. In addition, the German raider, *Doggerbank*, made its presence in South African waters known. (Aircraft launched from submarines?).

On 6th June the Japanese sank three ships, followed by another seven ships between 6 and 12 June. Admiral Ishizaki was having a field day in the Moçambique Channel. The first Japanese aircraft launched from a submarine flew over

Durban on 20th May. This was before the sinking's begun. It flew over at 05h15, its navigation lights on. Challenged by the Fire Commander of Durban Fortress Air Defence it gave the wrong letter of the day and disappeared out to sea. The Japanese made their closest approach to Durban on 5th June 1942.

On 25th May 1942, No 6 Squadron handed over five of its aircraft, including four Mohawks to No 10 Fighter Squadron. On 5th June 1942, Dad went solo on the Mohawk. On the 24th, the Squadron deployed to Stanger for five weeks and then to Isipingo for two months. The Stanger deployments were to provide air cover for shipping in the Moçambique Channel, as well as along the Zululand coastline. During June Dad added a Hawker Audax to his growing number of aircraft types, in addition to the Harvard and Mohawk with which No 10 Squadron was equipped. On 7th October, Dad returned to Roberts Heights (Voortrekkerhoogte) for five days for his next posting.

Hawker Audax

On 2nd September 1939 10 Fairey Battle squadrons flew to France
as the major offensive element of the Advanced Air Striking Force.
Facing the Blitzkrieg they were pumped into battle and suffered
severely from the Curtiss-fighters — in one attack 13 out of 15
failing to return.

Not Mohawk – but Fairey Battle

MusHavel MOHAWK IV (Curtiss H-75 A-4) 1/48 scale - ref. MH148001
MONTAGE / BUILD-UP : SÉBASTIEN DELETTE

Curtiss Mohawk

45 Air School - Oudshoorn

The Joint Air Training Scheme, formed at the end of 1940, established some 24 air schools in order to supply the necessary aircrew skills. These units, initially, were:

Elementary Flying Training — Baragwanath and Randfontein

Service Flying Training — Kimberley, Vereeniging, Waterkloof

Air Observers — East London, Port Elizabeth

Air Observers, Navigators — Oudtshoorn

Air Gunners, Air Observers and Navigators — Queenstown

Central Flying School — Bloemfontein

Ground Instruction — Bloemfontein

Air Armament — Youngsfield

Air Navigation — Youngsfield

Air Photography — Zwartkops

Technical Training — Roberts Heights, Zwartkops, Kimberly

Basic Training — Johannesburg, Port Elizabeth, Pretoria

Clerks and Storemen Air Crew Depot — Lyttleton

On 12th October 1942 Lieutenant Preller Geldenhuys reported to No 45 Air School in Oudshoorn, equipped with Avro Anson, twin-engined coastal reconnaissance/light bomber aircraft, and powered by A S Cheetah engines. Wing Commander 'Firpo' Chichester commanded 45 Air School. Flying Officer R W Bass (OC Instructional Flight) checked Dad out and on the 23rd Dad recorded his 1st Solo on type.

Anson – Big brother to the Airspeed Oxford

Piper Cub conversion

Before the month was out, Flying Officer Bass also instructed Dad on the Piper Cub, with the second 'first solo', in one month, being logged on October 30. The air station was constantly on the alert for attack by the 'OB' - Ossewabrandwag, bent on sabotage of aircraft, and security flights were regularly made in the Piper Cub to check the entrances to the valley through Calitzdorp, Meiringspoort and Montagu Pass. German U-boat offensives were taking a heavy toll. On October 9th, U-68 hit the American tanker *Swiftsure* south of Cape Point then sank the freighter *Sarthe*, followed by sinking the *Belgian Fighter* between Slangkop and Cape Town harbour. By the end of the month, U-177, U-

178 and U-181 rounded the Cape and sailed up the south-east coast. With more U-boats appearing, coastal patrols were stepped up.

Primary routes were to George, Port Elizabeth, Cape Seal and Riversdale. Other lesser known turning points included obscure places like Zwarts, Kivietskuil, Stydomsvlei, Seekoegatsvlei, Vondeling, Beenekraal, Windheuvel Poort, Three Sisters, Prince Albert, Miller, Nelspoort, Willowmore, Cactus Farm, Beaufort West, De Rust, Steytlerville, Rietbron, Merweville, Cape Infanta, Barrydale, Uniondale, Aberdeen, Mosselbay and Knysna. Phew - that was a mouthful - I didn't know there were so many places in the Cape.

Sorties were generally lengthy, of the order of three and half-hour duration. Crews also consisted of pilot plus four. Solo was only flown on first night solo. Some of the more memorable sorties include being sent out to sea on patrol, identifying a hospital ship during a sea sweep, and landing asymmetrically when the starboard engine ran rough and was shut-down, forced landing on 'drome'. I recall Dad recounting an experience of also being forced to land wheels-up - where he had the presence of mind to shut down both engines, and using the starter motor to turn the two bladed propellers to the horizontal alignment, so as not to damage the engines on belly-landing. Now that is keeping a cool head during an emergency. I might add that flying with only one engine is quite tricky - because power changes on the live engine causes a yawing motion, which in turn either lifts or drops a wing, necessitating flying the machine cross controls. As most pilots will tell you, cross control flying invites incipient spins - or flicking onto your back, which is "not so nice", as Rina would say.

On 20th February 1943 Preller Matt Geldenhuys was born on Rustpan, the family farm at Bothaville, Free State. It seems Dad took leave of absence from 12th February to 9th March.

On 22nd March 1943, Lieutenant P Geldenhuys added Fairey Battle No 921 to his record of aircraft types. He had left Port

Elizabeth for Port Alfred two days earlier for his dual conversion. The return to Port Elizabeth was by Airspeed Oxford, which is not unlike the Anson. Two days later he flew a Battle along the coast all the way from Port Elizabeth to Oudtshoorn. In May, he flew a Battle to Cape Town with his crew of Captain Davis and WO Harper, to return with a Major Corlewis after a couple of night stops.

Fairey Battle light bomber
Bomb load: 680 Kg
Max speed: 406 Km/h

6:17 / 10:11

Oudad flew a total of 103 hours in the 'Battle' – a rather cumbersome aircraft to handle

By the end of 1943, South Africa had suffered 30,000 casualties, of whom some 5,400 had been killed or died on service and about 14,000 were languishing in prisoner-of-war camps. The number of ships sunk, damaged or captured by enemy raiders and submarines in South African coastal waters rose from only 16 between the outbreak of war and the end 1941, to 85 during 1942. During 1943 the number was 54.

Delene Elizabeth Geldenhuys was born in Oudtshoorn on 27th February 1945.

On May 24th, Flying Officer Bass again carried out a dual check in Oxford 20, sending Dad off on a solo flight. In June, Lieutenant P Geldenhuys was allocated to the Battle Flight, commanded by Squadron Leader S O'Grady - for a spell of flying instruction. His Battle pupil pilots were Lieutenants Bard, Thomson, van Wezel, Williams, Sergeant Hammond, Corporals Honan, Stone, and LACs Dinning and Rogers. Bombing and target towing instruction was given. By September 1943, Lieutenant Preller Geldenhuys was appointed Officer Commanding 'Battle' Flight, to Flight Lieutenant R Bass as Officer Commanding 45 Air Squadron, Oudtshoorn. By end October, Dad had flown with 612 passengers/crew, and had flown in 19 different aircraft types.

Airspeed Oxford
(NZ Oxford – Christchurch Museum)

Lieutenant Preller Geldenhuys remained Officer Commanding Battle Flight until the end of November 1943, and was then converted fully on the Oxford, qualifying as first pilot (night) on 17th January 1944. He then alternated between the Anson and Oxford Flights, flying both types as a "staff bombing pilot". He then did a short two-month spell with No 44 Air School at Grahamstown, followed by a stint with No 43 Air School at Port Alfred.

43 Air School – Port Alfred / 68 AS

Adolf Hitler had committed suicide on 30th April 1945, with Germany forces in Italy surrendering on 2nd May. The War in Europe ended on 8th May 1945. On August 6th, the first atomic bomb was dropped on Hiroshima, on the 8th, Russia declared war on Japan, on the 9th the second atomic bomb was dropped on Nagasaki and on 14th August 1945, Emperor Hirohito announced Japan's surrender. World War II ended on the 15th August 1945.

On 9th October 1945, Lieutenant Preller Geldenhuys was posted to 68 AS Lyttelton for a month and released from the SAAF at Hector Norris Park on 7th November 1945. Shortly after his de-mobilisation, Dad packed his bags and immigrated with his young family to Northern Rhodesia – to become a miner on the Copperbelt. The pioneer spirit of Abram Carl Fredrik Preller Geldenhuys, to trek north, will be continued shortly. In the interim, it is evident that other 'distant relatives' also contributed to the war effort.

The following members of the Geldenhuys family served in, and gave their lives, during World War II. Captain M Geldenhuys was a pilot serving on No 3 Squadron, South African Air Force, on 10th November 1943. The squadron was based at Savoia, Eastern Mediterranean, and tasked with convoy protection and shipping standby as 25 ships and five escorts were passing en route Bengasi. He was one of six Hurricane II Cs pilots scrambled to intercept six Junker 88s and five Dornier 217s escorted by five fighters about to attack the ship convoy. A Captain R Yeats attacked two Ju 88s and sent one down, but after attacking another his screen frosted up and he lost contact with the enemy in the gathering darkness. A second Hurricane pilot fired at a Ju88 and saw it crash into the sea but did not claim a share. Captain M Geldenhuys led his section into an attack during which the pilots individually fired bursts at four Ju 88s, one of which went into the sea. Another lost height, with port engine smoking and a Do 217 was also destroyed. The enemy single-engined aircraft made no attempt to intervene before the engagement had to be broken off because of darkness.

Much later, during October 1944, No 3 Squadron SAAF, as part of No 8 Wing, was based at Borghetto (Near Ancona and Florence, Italy), and by now equipped with Spitfire aircraft. Captain M Geldenhuys is again mentioned as playing his full part in 8 Wing activities, in leading missions either against designated targets or on cab-rank patrol.

Petty Officer J C M Geldenhuys served in the South Africa Naval Service at the outbreak of World War II. South Africa possessed no real naval vessels on the outbreak of war, but their strength consisted of three officers and three ratings. Geldenhuys was subordinate to Lieutenant Commanders J Dalgleish and F J Dean. More research is needed to establish his relationship.

For interest, Geldenhuys combatants that did not survive World War II were: Warrant Officer Class II G J Geldenhuys, of No 15 Squadron, Royal Air Force, was posted missing, presumed dead (drowned at sea). Geldenhuys was the third crew member of a Baltimore bomber, piloted by Lieutenant. D B Dick. On 30th January 1945, No 15 Squadron's Baltimore, with a crew of four, disappeared on a night cross-country flight. A Boston aircraft reported seeing a fire at sea, and eventually a rescue launch off Bellaria picked up three Mae Wests, two of which belonged to No 15 Squadron. The missing aircrews were Lieutenants D B Dick and W E Ellis, Warrant Officer G J Geldenhuys and Sergeant Slaughter of the RAF, reported lost.

By a strange twist of fate, 15 Squadrons first loss since February 1944 was suffered during the Baltimore's final operation before standing down on 19th January. OC Lieutenant Colonel Shuttleworth led the mission of nine aircraft to attack a stores dump at Massa Lombarda, where they met with intense heavy anti-aircraft fire. His port engine was set on fire. The Baltimore was crash-landed about 16 km from base - at Casenatico. WO II G J Geldenhuys was thus lost at sea, after the squadron had stood down eleven days earlier.

Warrant Officer Class II, J N Geldenhuys, was killed in action during the closing stages of World War II. It is speculated that his initials stood for Johannes Norval. J N Geldenhuys was a crew member on a Liberator of No 34 Squadron, South African Air Force, piloted by Captain L J de Jager that was hit by flak during their bombing run on Villach. Villach was a key point on the railway line into Austria, which was attacked twice within four days. 50 heavies were very successful on the night of 25/26 March 1945, when the goods and transhipment depots were almost totally destroyed. Unfortunately, the flak was accurate. The Liberator was manned by pilot plus a crew of eight. The members of the crew killed in action were Lieutenants R L Chegwyn, P M Tylden-Wright, I J Doble, Flying Officer R Warrington, WOs J N Geldenhuys, J Robbertse and W A J Venter, and Sergeant A C Phillips. G J and J N Geldenhuys relationships still need to be established. Genealogy research is still incomplete and I trust their connections will be determined in due course.

World War 2 Campaign medals

Summary of Aircraft Types and Hours

(Oudad's Flying Logbook)

AIRCRAFT TYPE	S.E. Aircraft	M.E. Aircraft
AVRO ANSON	-	680.30
AIRSPEED OXFORD	-	110.25
FAIREY BATTLE	106.30	-
D.H. TIGER MOTH	98.25	-
GLOSTER GLADIATOR	66.40	-
HAWKER HIND	63.40	-
N.A. HARVARD	58.45	-
PIPER CUB	28.30	-
HAWKER HART	19.40	-
LOCKHEED LODESTAR	18.45	-
PIPER CRUISER	15.00	-
CURTISS P36 MOHAWK	10.35	-
SHORT SUNDERLAND		8.55

93

Back cover of the Nickel Cross Book

SAAF Interlude - Great North Road

World War II ended on the 15th August 1945, on my brother Jan's fifth birthday. Dad last flew with 'A' Flight, No 43 Air School, in Harvard 7342 on 29th August - having logged 1,231 hours and 15 minutes. He completed his tour with 43 Air School on 8th October 1945, having flown 16 types, and was released from the SAAF as Lieutenant on 7th November 1945.

Although my ancestors were farmers, and Dad had inherited the "familie plaas Rustpan", he was reluctant to return to farming as a career. He ceded his inheritance to his brother-in-law Steyn Jordaan and persuaded my Mom to head for the Great North Road - or at least to Northern Rhodesia - and give copper mining a go as a trail-busting career.

Copperbelt - Northern Rhodesia

By the end of the following year, my parents had settled at Luanshya with Dad as a miner with the Roan Antelope Copper Mine. Pioneering prospector William Collier discovered copper deposits in 1902 in what became one of the world's richest copper-producing countries. The Copperbelt mining towns, from north to south, are Bancroft, Chingola, Mufulira, Chambishi, Chibuluma, Kitwe and Luanshya. The Refinery and administrative centre was at Ndola. Dad mined at Roan Antelope (Luanshya) and Nchanga (Chingola). All of the larger towns had flying clubs. But it was not long before he got his bum in the air again, going solo in Piper Cub VP-RBG on my fifth birthday – 20th February 1948. However I had to wait until 15th July for my first air experience. Dad's first passenger was Willem Boshoff, followed by Master Jan and Master Preller Geldenhuys.

At that age, I presume I was privileged to have defied gravity even before starting schooling. What I do recall however, is that the "g" forces terrified me whereas my brother Jan certainly loved it - the sortie lived up to its callsign - not phonetically "Bravo Golf" but "Bak Gat". My brother Jan took to the air like a duck to water.

The following day, my sister Delene, who was then only 3 years old, enjoyed her first air experience (and according to Dad's log books) so much so that she became a regular "hog" - in Air Force jargon, hogging the hours.

Anyway, during the ensuing year, the Geldenhuys children became regular aviators. I enjoyed no fewer than eight sorties and logging up numerous types to my credit, namely Piper Cub, Cruiser, Voyager and a Stinson.

A break of eight years followed, and by 1957 my parents moved to Chingola with Dad now mining at Nchanga Copper Mines Ltd. By July of that year Dad had joined the Chingola Flying Club, and I, the Boy Scouts. It was not long before I again enjoyed flying and logged up another couple of sorties.

Being an intrepid aviator, and a keen Boy Scout I soon set about earning as many Proficiency Badges as I could - and it was not long before I achieved the dubious distinction of being one of the first Copperbelt Scouts to be awarded the Airmanship Badge. Since there were no Air Scouts there at the time, the Badge had to be sent for from Lusaka before the presentation could be made. With my Dad being an active Flying Club member, I had the added advantage of being schooled by my father in the rudiments of Airmanship, and could put into practice the marshalling of the light aircraft operations at the aerodromes. I'm sure Dad was very proud of me for being the first recipient of the Boy Scout's Airmanship award on the Copperbelt.

Dawnie Geldenhuys

Dawnie was the first Rhodesian born Geldenhuys. Dawnie, our youngest sister, was born at Luanshya in 1949, and had just grown out of babyhood when my father transferred to Chingola and bought ten acres at Musenga Plots, some ten miles out of town.

One Friday evening, 13th August 1954, a Swahili set fire to our thatched cottage which was occupied at that time only by my elder brother Jan, my sister Delene and six year old Dawnie. Jan and Delene survived the inferno - Dawnie didn't. Jan had woken up to the sound of a gunshot. It was the gun my father had kept next to his bed. The bedroom section curtains had caught alight and the heat had caused the gun to go off. The thatched cottage was filled with smoke and as Jan got down from the top bunk bed, he roused my younger sister Delene from her slumber - no doubt because of the carbon dioxide effect of all the smoke. He searched the bottom bunk bed for my little sister Dawn, but could not find nor see her. He concluded that she had already vacated the bed and was most probably already outside because of the intense heat within the cottage. Jan then dragged Delene out of the raging fire and once outside tried in vain to locate our youngest sister. By this time the thatched roof had collapsed in, and the heat and fire from the thatch so intense that it was impossible to attempt re-entering the burning cottage. In fact, had he done so, he would not have survived the attempt.

The Geldenhuys family, in Chingola, Northern Rhodesia

My parents were visiting me at that time, having been hospitalised with Malaria. They had gone to catch a movie before Dad went on night shift, while Mom returned to the plot - only to be confronted by the tragic events of that unlucky Friday the 13th.

A Swahili from up North was the prime suspect. The Swahili, who had been recruited as a domestic on one of our frequent fishing trips to the lakes - Tanganyika, Bangwelo and Mrewa - was never brought to justice for his arson. He was thought to have set our caravan and several thatched rondavels alight at weekly or fortnightly intervals. The police would post a guard at the plot, but has soon as the police presence was withdrawn, a further incident would occur. These fires continued for quite a while, and the police was quite useless in taking the culprit into custody, despite all the incriminating evidence.

The loss of Dawnie caused my mother to have several bouts of severe depression - the worst being when she put a revolver under her chin and pulled the trigger - and was fortunately saved by her false teeth. The round deflected off the bottom set, shattered the top plate and exited via the mouth. Apart from having her broken jaw wired up, Mum was indeed lucky to survive the suicide attempt.

I am pleased to record that Mom survived untold "All Things Bright and Beautiful, All Things Great and Small" thereafter, (the tune was Dawn's favourite) - and even outlived my father. Today's date is Friday 13th August 1999 - precisely 45 years ago to the day - that I edited this work. It is perhaps by Divine Intervention, rather than pure coincidence, that I had occasion to witness this tragic event in the Geldenhuys household. Dawnie has been in my thoughts all day. I trust God, in all his wisdom, that the heavenly Angels continue to protect and keep her from all evil, and that God's mercy will continue to shine his light on our offspring in memory of a beautiful lost one. By the time our grandchildren read this, I trust that they would at least live to experience and see out 45 years.

All of the A C F Preller Geldenhuys children had their early schooling on the Copperbelt towns of Luanshya and Chingola. It even included a Convent school, although our schooling was mainly at Government schools.

To get to Lake Tanganyika from Fort Roseberry, we would travel to Luwingu, Kasama, Abercorn, and then take the treacherous Great Rift Valley road down to the Mpulungu port settlement. Abercorn was the nearest sizeable town to the lake. There is a beautiful waterfall near Luwingu. I remember an occasion when my Dad caught a leguaan by the tail – the reptile is extremely agile and just catching it as it scurried towards the lake was no mean feat. Lake Tanganyika was described in the Horizon as one of the deepest – and most beautiful – lakes in the world. It came thus as no surprise why my Dad had decided to immigrate to the Copperbelt en route to North Africa during World War II.

Jan and I hitchhiked from the Copperbelt to spend time on a farm at Fort Victoria, Southern Rhodesia. It was not long thereafter that my father decided to pack up mining to go farming instead - to Stanmore farm outside Fort Victoria.

Southern Rhodesia

My father bought an old Bedford lorry for the household removals from Chingola to Stanmore farm and also to commence farming with. His life savings from mining were used up to buy seed, an old second hand Fordson tractor and basic farming implements. Our first crop of mielies, kaffircorn and castor oil seeds was a disaster. The second crop was not much better.

Farming was not a bed of roses and it was not long before Dad was forced to seek supplementary employment - building the road that leads to Kyle Dam. Not only did he do this with distinction but also received a gratuity for designing an instrument for blasting the approach road to the dam wall site through the granite kopjies which is a natural feature in the Kyle landscape.

Meanwhile on the farm, our fortunes declined resulting in my parents settling back in South Africa where my father started selling insurance for Old Mutual in Bothaville. It was not long before he returned to mining at Orkney.

Rejoined SAAF

Having his son join the Royal Rhodesian Air Force prompted Dad to re-join the South African Air Force. By this time he was too old for flying duties but willingly accepted a mustering to Storeman.

No sooner was UDI declared in Rhodesia that Dad joined S.T.T. at Lyttleton twelve days later on the 23rd November 1965. Whereas the Unilateral Declaration of Independence was a hectic period for the country to the north of South Africa, just so was it south of the border at Pretoria where uniform was donned once again and settling into Air Force routines, till the sixteenth December of 1965.

10 Air Depot – Voortrekkerhoogte

Dad spent all of the next six years at 10 AD V.T.H., Pretoria. He was happy there, he was good at his job and very well-liked by all – both in and out of uniform. He even had his leg pulled when I used to visit him at his office, driving through the security booms with the Rhodesian Attaché governments' staff car during Operation Hottentot (Sanctions busting and flying SAAF Vampires back to Rhodesia). 10 AD was basically across the Waterkloof runway.

Dad was barely back in uniform for four months when the writer married his high school sweetheart. Dad motored up from Pretoria, with his sister Aunt Minnie van Rensen, to attend the wedding.

1965 was the start of the 15-year Rhodesian War 1965 – 1980. The photograph taken at the wedding reminded the writer of the photograph taken of Dad, his elder brother and our Grand-father, at the start of this story – his World War II story.

Dad died in uniform – at Voortrekkerhoogte Military Hospital, on the 13th February 1972.

Preller Geldenhuys – Junior and Senior – In Air Force No One Blues, March 1966

Bibliography

Geldenhuys, Abram Carl Frederik Preller, *Pilots Flying Logbook.*

Geldenhuys, Lizzie, *Oorlogsherinneringe van Lizzie Geldenhuys*

Becker, Dave, *Yellow Wings,* SAAF Museum, 1989

Becker, Dave, *The Eagles of Zwartkop* (Freeworld Publications 1996)

Brent, Winston, *Rhodesian Air Force – The Sanction Busters* (Freeworld Publications 2001)

S.A. Air Force Golden Jubilee Souvenir Book - 1970

Scannell, Ted, *Aviation in Central Africa*, (Horizon, 1960)

Schoeman, Michael, *Springbok Fighter Victory*, (2002)

Index

105

www.ingramcontent.com/pod-product-compliance
Lightning Source LLC
Chambersburg PA
CBHW030957090426
42737CB00007B/571